THE FOREVER HOME

THE FOREVER HOME

MIKEL WELCH

*Classic, Clever Design
to Help You Put Down Roots*

PRINCIPAL PHOTOGRAPHY BY ERIN AUSTEN ABBOTT

Clarkson Potter/Publishers
New York

To my mother, Kathy, who told me, "Follow your passion. You'll know what it is because it will be something you'd be willing to do for free." That statement was short but powerful, and it changed the entire trajectory of my career. Without her, there would be no Mikel Welch Designs—no me, no business, no purpose.

CONTENTS

FOREWORD BY SHEA MCGEE 9
FOREWORD BY DREW BARRYMORE 13

INTRODUCTION:
MY FOREVER HOME
JOURNEY

17

SPACE AND STYLE
PLANNING

25

SET THE MOOD
41

FIND COLOR BALANCE
81

EMPHASIZE THE DETAILS
121

PICK THE RIGHT FURNISHINGS
193

RESOURCES 256
ACKNOWLEDGMENTS 264
PHOTO CREDITS 266
INDEX 267

FOREWORD

by Shea McGee

Long before Studio McGee *appeared alongside words like* Netflix *and* Target, and before kids, companies, and contracts, I was a twenty-three-year-old newlywed in a one-bedroom apartment dreaming of my future forever home. I painted the cabinets in our tiny rental kitchen and finessed the layout with secondhand and gifted furniture until the flow felt just right from one corner of the 600-square-foot apartment to the other. I still have items that I tucked away in the little storage space we had there, knowing that one day they'd have the perfect place in a home that was all ours. Years later, after launching Studio McGee, moving states, and living in a few more rentals—and with two (of our eventual three) young girls in tow—my husband, Syd, and I stood in an empty dirt lot in a neighborhood of Salt Lake City known for its views of the Wasatch Mountains and watched a hole being dug and a foundation poured; layer by layer, our forever home took shape. As the raw framing of the walls went up, we talked about the little things that would make it ours—a backyard where Syd could grill, and a pantry (painted in my favorite shade of green) for all my baking ingredients. By the time we had the keys, I had designed every inch of the house in my mind, a pinboard full of samples and swatches outlining the design direction in each room; finally, I was my own client. A lot of my meticulous planning was about color theory, juxtaposition of materials, and space planning rather than pillows and wallpaper. As someone putting down roots in their family's forever home, I wanted to create a space that would hold what could be a lifetime of memories, and that space needed to function properly and flow with ease, with room to grow and high livability. The design decisions I made were all prefaced by the word *forever*, and quickly followed by the word *phases*. I knew getting it just right would take time, not only due to budget and bandwidth constraints, but because making decisions that will last is much easier when you've lived in the home—watched how the sun comes in through the windows, noticed where day-to-day stuff piles up, and observed the nuances of seamlessly getting a family of five out the door on a Monday morning during the school year. Some things in a new build, like the type of flooring, need to be decided on at the start, while others, like a bold wallpaper or an area rug, are over-time decisions that are best made after getting to know the space. In this book, Mikel beautifully defines the intricacies of the decisions that are prefaced with "forever" and leads us through crafting a home that is just as much a part of the memories that are lived inside it as the people who live them. To me, the sense of a "forever home" has nothing to do with whether you live in it for the rest of your life or hand it down to your children or a stranger, but rather with the sense of safety and permanence you feel inside it. Its walls house your personal legacy, if only for a short time, and the moments that are etched in your memory forever.

The Art of Home

Written by Shea McGee

FOREWORD

by Drew Barrymore

I am so excited to be writing this foreword because I love this man! When I first met Mikel Welch, I quickly realized we shared a deep passion for creating spaces that are both beautiful and deeply personal. Mikel's approach to design is about more than just aesthetics—it's about crafting homes that reflect the unique stories and needs of the families who live in them. He has an incredible ability to listen, understand, and transform a space into something that feels truly authentic.

Together, we've collaborated on countless design projects, always with the same goal in mind: to create homes that are a reflection of the people who inhabit them. Whether it's a family just starting out or one looking to make their home a true sanctuary, Mikel's designs always prioritize comfort, warmth, and the feeling of belonging. The spaces we create are not just rooms; they're places where memories are made, a home that tells a story and evolves with the people who live there.

I trust Mikel's judgment completely. His keen eye for design, combined with his understanding of what truly makes a home special, is not only why I asked him to be the resident interior designer on the talk show that has my name on it, but also because I always wanted it to be a place for experts to be able to collaborate with people who I trust and admire. Mikel and I were peas in a design pod since day one. He has an incredible way of bringing creativity, humor, and heart into every project, and I love getting to work side by side with him to elevate spaces and try to bring beauty to people in their important and personal spaces.

In his book, Mikel shares his approach to creating the Forever Home—spaces that are designed to grow with you and stand the test of time. I'm so proud to be part of his journey, and I can't wait for you to experience the beauty and soul he brings to every design. He is also the most wonderful human. An asset in every single way. And now he has made a book. Lucky for us, we get to continue to learn from his knowledge and be inspired by his talents.

And so we begin.

Happy reading.

Opposite: And that's a wrap!

Opposite: Catching a glimpse of Drew taping live just before I join her onstage for a segment on *The Drew Barrymore Show.*

INTRODUCTION

MY FOREVER HOME JOURNEY

Some say a "forever home" is a place we're meant to stay, well, forever. But I take a less literal approach: to me, the forever home is for everyone, regardless of circumstance. Just because you may not be living in a space long-term—maybe you are a renter or plan to move again after a few years—doesn't mean you don't deserve to have a place that's all yours. A home doesn't have to break the bank to be beautiful. It doesn't have to have high-end designer pieces to feel whole and loved. Our homes should bring joy to our everyday lives and reflect our personalities, whether through major structural changes or something as simple as removable wallpaper. From the coffee table we select to the art we hang on the walls, every element tells a story, imbuing our homes with character and soul.

Whether you're having brunch with friends or on a dream trip to a far-off location, your home should always welcome you back with a sense of familiarity and warmth. It's more than just a physical space—it's the backdrop to your life, an expression of who you are and what matters most to you.

My forever home journey has seen me crisscross the country through seven states and even more homes, each of which I have made my own. Your journey might look different from mine. You may be building your dream house, or you may be a renter with a new address every few years. Either way, you deserve a forever home.

After you read this book, I want you to feel empowered to make design selections that previously would have left you paralyzed with decision fatigue. I want you to feel good investing in a high-end piece while also celebrating your low-end finds. I want you to feel confident letting your personality shine through, creating a home that tells your unique story and supports the way you live. Most of all, I want you to feel good from the moment you step inside. At the end of the day, a true forever home is defined not by the way it looks but by the way it makes you feel.

Just Getting Started

I was the second oldest of four, growing up in Detroit, Michigan. Our parents cultivated an environment that sparked creativity and imagination while encouraging us to follow our passions. My mother was a TV news journalist and the on-air traffic reporter and weatherperson for many years. She also hosted a local TV show, while my father started out as a disc jockey. I've had entertainment in my blood from a young age.

As a child, I always had an interest in architecture. I spent hours creating tiny communities with LEGO bricks and Fisher-Price people, honing my appreciation for design and providing the building blocks (no pun intended) for what my career would become.

After graduating from Morehouse College in Atlanta, Georgia, with a BA in marketing, I bounced from job to job in furniture sales and store merchandising, never feeling quite settled in my work. I kept circling back to my passion for design and the tiny communities of my childhood. I had also found a new love of rearranging my house, as well as the homes of friends and anyone else in my circles who would let me get my hands on their space. I would hit up the thrift shops and discount stores weekly, looking for items I could transform into high-end looks on my shoestring budget.

How Craigslist Changed My Life

Starting a business without any clients meant I needed to turn to my marketing degree and get creative. To build a portfolio, as a side hustle from my furniture sales job, I became my own client, redesigning my apartment and getting it professionally photographed. In the early days of Craigslist, I made an ad offering to design one room for free if people paid for the furniture. And you know what? It worked. I began to get clients. I would design one room for free, and if they liked it, they could pay me to design a second or third room. To help keep costs down and further my goal of designing full-time, I would handle the small jobs, like painting, myself (being so hands-on equipped me with invaluable home renovation skills that serve me well to this day).

The more clients I acquired, the more deeply I fell in love with designing spaces. *Could this be the direction of my career?* I thought.

A showhouse is a curated event where multiple designers are each assigned a room within a single home that they transform to showcase their unique style. These spaces are displayed to the public for a limited time. Designers often use these homes to attract new clients and press coverage.

One thing I really love about designing for showhouses is that I can realize my vision for the space without worrying about what the client thinks. It's my time to get creative and share ideas. I'm allowed to take risks and push the boundaries a little, such as by using my DIY version of chalk limewash (found on page 117).

My Big Break

I always had my mother's voice in my head telling me I needed to find my passion. Well, it found me when one day, when a set decorator came into the furniture store. I made it my business to approach anyone who looked like they might be a designer and ask them questions about getting started. I also made a point to ask whether I could possibly shadow them on a project. You'd be surprised how willing people are to help when they realize that you don't want anything from them other than just to learn. On that particular day, I must have asked the right questions, or showed the correct amount of gumption, because the designer offered me a job as a production assistant on a TV show.

You better be sure I jumped at that opportunity! I finally had my foot in the door. Which lead me to eventually begin working on designer showhouses.

The quick, transformative, and temporary nature of this design work gave me the skills to create eye-catching designs in a variety of rooms on a tight timeline. Think of showhouses as pop-up shops for the interior design world. Much like the work on a TV show set. It provided a remarkable foundation for my life's direction for the next twenty years.

Chasing the Dream

In the span of a year, I learned so much from designing for showhouses, including how to conduct a consultation, give a client presentation, and put together a budget. I got my feet wet and gained the knowledge I would need to one day start my own interior design firm. I had big plans for the future, but I knew I needed more experience before taking that leap. So I continued to accept freelance projects, building my portfolio and reputation.

Then one day, while assisting at a jobsite, I crossed paths with Jillian Browder, Director of Creative Services for Dior brands. A visual merchandiser, interior designer, and photo stylist, she would become my mentor. She threw me a lifeline, inviting me to collaborate. One of my first projects with Jillian was assisting her on a designer showhouse that was on a completely different tier than any I'd previously worked on. I had taken a step up from middle-of-the-road to full-on luxury (I'm talking $30,000 rugs), where everything was custom. I'd come a long way from my early Craigslist projects. After working with Jillian for a few years, I briefly returned to furniture sales before landing jobs with *Teen Vogue* as an unpaid intern and as a production assistant on Emily Henderson's show *Secrets from a Stylist*, just after her win on *Design Star*. From there, I moved to Esquire Network (formerly Style Network). I had to shift gears quickly and learn to create makeshift drawings as my visuals, which are sort of like 3D blueprints. Visuals tell the carpenters what your vision for the design is and are a critical part of the TV set design process. I had to acquire this skill seemingly overnight, both drawing by hand and teaching myself to use PowerPoint. The renderings helped me visualize each set before moving forward with the design. Sometimes creating the rendering helped me realize that the design in my mind wouldn't translate into real life. It was a learning curve that I was willing to follow fast.

Finally, after years of honing my craft behind the scenes, I decided to step into the spotlight and audition for HGTV *Design Star*. And guess what? I got the part! I was cast as a contestant on the show and finished in fourth place. The rest is history, as they say.

Working on HGTV *Design Star* opened a lot of doors for me. In 2014, I designed a room for a showhouse in the home of the late John Hughes, director of the iconic films *Ferris Bueller's Day Off*, *The Breakfast Club*, *Home Alone*, and *Sixteen Candles*. That led to my landing my first features in *Architectural Digest* and *Elle Decor*.

I've since worked on the sets for more than nine TV shows, including *The Steve Harvey Show*, *The Drew Barrymore Show*, *Jerseylicious*, *Harry*, *Trading Spaces*, and *Design Star*. I've worked with Sherée Whitfield of *The Real Housewives of Atlanta*; on the Faith Hill–produced show *Pickler & Ben*, starring Kellie Pickler and Ben Aaron; and as a cohost of the Emmy-winning Netflix show *Hack My Home*.

Clockwise from the top: Getting camera-ready for the *The Drew Barrymore Show*. Everything must be styled just right so the cameras can pick up each detail. Drew and me on a segment discussing easy, affordable ways to collect art.

21

I've designed sets and rooms for Martha Stewart, Nate Berkus, the Property Brothers, Michelle Obama, Oprah Winfrey, Halle Berry, Joan Rivers, Bishop T. D. Jakes, Tyler Perry, Kathie Lee Gifford, and Hoda Kotb.

Today, I work as a member of the Drew Crew on *The Drew Barrymore Show*, appearing on camera for various segments on topics such as design, thrifting, and organizing. I've even filled in and cohosted the entire show. I also continue to run my own interior design business for private clients and do home design consulting for Lincoln Motor Company customers through their points perks system and the website The Expert. I'm happy where I am, but also feel like my story is just getting started. Which is exciting! This book is part of my journey. I can't wait to see where we go together.

So How Do You Get This Forever Home I'm Speaking Of?

Much of what I've learned is from years of trial and error (you can be sure I've made plenty of mistakes . . . thank goodness for learning curves) and from creating countless TV sets. On the typical talk show, each guest requires a new design, forcing me to think quickly and far outside the box, while operating on a shoestring budget. Despite all the restrictions, each transition has to look seamless— and it always does, thanks to smoke and mirrors (see my tips related to that concept throughout).

Sets are always in a constant state of rotation and last a short time before they are disassembled and reimagined.

I'm going to let you in on a little secret from *The Drew Barrymore Show* that you would have never guessed from looking at the stylish and well-put-together sets: we often "dumpster dive" to make these looks happen! When I don't have the budget or time to scour Craigslist or Facebook Marketplace, I will walk the two- or three-block radius of the studio to see what I can find. People often throw out great, gently used furniture on the streets of New York City (and in most cities in the United States). It's just a matter of knowing when the large-item dump nights are, and you can find some fantastic pieces. For free! I once found a nearly perfect dresser, which just needed a little paint. This is an excellent example of how we can create a high-end look at home without breaking the budget.

You may have already figured out that my thought process is rougher than an average designer's. I don't follow the typical design handbook. Instead, I look for moments within the design that give you pause and invite you to sit a bit longer with the look and feel of it. I integrate affordability and durability with long-lasting pieces. I feel that when creating your forever home, the items you put in it are as important as the structure itself.

I want to teach you the art of illusion with behind-the-scenes secrets and tangible advice. You can work magic even with only a local-thrift-shop and big-box-store budget. You don't have to live in a large urban center to achieve the designs you see in print or on TV.

Whether you have purchased a home or not, it is still *your* home, wherever you make it.

Over the years, I have rearranged, painted, and redesigned more times than I can count, both on-set and with clients, and learned how to blend high-end and low-end pieces. I want to share the knowledge I've gained so your home can come together with ease and grace—while looking stunning in the process. I want to teach you how to collect beloved pieces for your home and share tips for a seamless remodel.

I want to give you the quick-change tools I've developed through my work in the TV world but allow you time to walk through your space and make decisions with a bit more deliberation.

As a self-taught designer, I have been in your shoes, figuring out where to start, where to look, and what to do. Think of this book as a textbook, your guide to creating a space that feels distinctively yours, whether in a home you can stay in forever or in a series of rentals.

I always carry my idea of a forever home with me wherever I move. It can be a fluid concept. By the end of this book, you will know how to create your forever home, no matter how stationary. This book is for renters, adult children moving back in with their parents, first-time homeowners, short-stay dwellers, dreamers of the someday home, *and* those who have already found the home they plan to stay in forever. I'm so glad you're along for the ride.

Let's jump in and get to work!

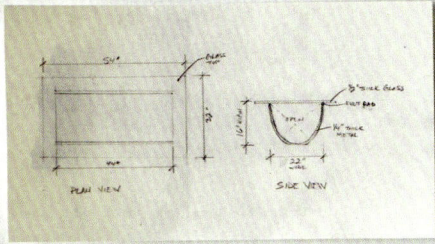

PLAN VIEW · SIDE VIEW

HIGH BACK CHAIR

Mikel Welch

DINING TABLE

Mikel Welch

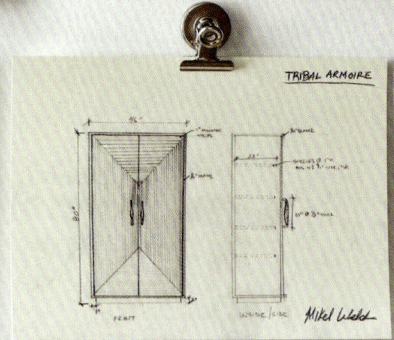

TRIBAL ARMOIRE

Mikel Welch

STOOL

Mikel Welch

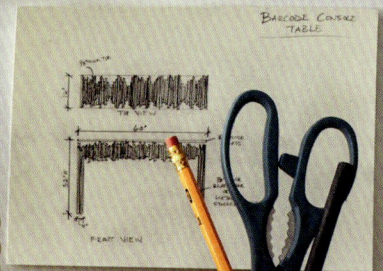

BAXCOOR COUSXRE TABLE

SPACE AND STYLE PLANNING

The average person doesn't have thousands of dollars to spend on building a new home or renovating their existing one. But with a little creative planning on the front end, you can still have a magazine-worthy look, and honey, we can even go to a big-box store to shop.

Before we dive in, let's address a few questions:

What does it mean to plan your space?
Why is space planning so important?
How do you get started?

When moving into a home, whether new construction or new-to-us, renting or owning, our first instinct is to buy things we love right away. I understand that impulse, but before you purchase any decor, art, or furnishings, you need to plan how items will fit into your space.

Space planning is the most essential part of the interior design process—I will walk you through creating a space-planning binder, which will essentially become your design bible. Maybe this sounds like overkill, and you just want to start shopping, but hear me out and you'll see how space planning will save you time, money, and energy. If you don't believe me, let me tell you a story. I have worked on a lot of shows, but I've never had the executive producer get down in the trenches with the crew like the one and only Mrs. Faith Hill. She was incredibly hands-on with the design process for the set of *Pickler & Ben*, once showing up with three three-ring binders. I'm not talking about skinny little ½-inch or 1-inch binders, but the large 2-inch binders, each meticulously organized by items in her home, her storage unit, and her second home. If she owned it, it was in a binder. Everything was labeled, measured, and photographed, including items she wanted to incorporate into the set. Anytime we needed something for the set, we were able to turn to her binders, which was a great help. It was like having our own warehouse at our disposal.

Your design bible does not need to be fancy. Mrs. Hill's was not fancy. It just needs to work for your needs.

You may be wondering why you should bother to compile a design bible if you are a renter. It's a great way to record the

Opposite: My mood board and thought process when planning a room. I like to lay out swatches, samples, drawings, and tear sheets to give the room a visual direction.

measurements of your sofa, headboard, table, and any other large pieces of furniture you have. You can also tuck paint samples into the binder sleeves, save tear sheets of rooms you admire in magazines, and so on. It's never too early to start planning your forever home. What if you move into a rental where the landlord allows you to paint the walls? You will be ready with colors you are drawn to. Maybe you'll find a new apartment with beautiful windows and a nice flow, but will your sofa fit in the living room? Will your bed make it down the hallway? You can answer these questions quickly with a design bible.

Your design bible is the key to creating your very organized forever home, and you should carry it with you whenever you work on your design. Giving yourself the time to properly space plan also allows you to chart any contracting issues that you may be up against later. For example, suppose you decide to add a TV to a given room after all the electrical work is complete, but you have no outlets available on the only wall where the TV will fit. In that case, you will cost yourself more time and money, which the budget might not allow for.

Everyone must know what they're walking into, whether you do the work yourself or hire it out.

Your space plan is vital for several reasons:

It will keep you on task. We often get excited when we see a piece of furniture or art we love, but whether you're making over your home entirely or designing one room at a time, having your space plan will keep you on track to look only for items that will fit in your space. Think about that sofa you might love in a magazine spread but which would never actually suit your needs. It's easier to let go of items when you know the exact size you need and what will work and what won't.

It will help you stay on budget. A space plan will help you prioritize your budget, room by room. We all like saving money, right?

It will make you work smarter. If you've never had to think about a space plan before, it's hard to know everything that should go into these early planning stages. Remember to measure everything. Save your paint colors, inspiration ideas, budget tracker, contracts and price quotes from hired workers, appliance manuals and warranties, floor plan, and numbers for plumbers, painters, electricians, and other tradespeople. Include a spot for jotting down notes and anything that comes to mind that you might need to record in your binder.

Pulling your space plan together isn't the most fun task, and along the way, it might feel like I've given you homework. Well, I have. This is literally home*work*. In the way that I hear the voice of my parents who pushed me to be better, I want you to hear my voice every time you overlook a detail that belongs in your binder. I don't want to have to say I told you so.

- PowerPoint
- Canva
- Private Pinterest board
- Private saved board on Instagram

WAYS TO KEEP YOUR SPACE
PLANNING ORGANIZED

- In a three-ring binder
- With the Notes app on your smartphone
- On a spreadsheet broken down by rooms in your home

Getting Started

I started out creating space plans with PowerPoint but have since upgraded to Canva. It's an inexpensive, if not free, way to build the vision for the space you see for yourself. You can also use platforms like Pinterest or Pages. When you find furnishings you love, drag a picture to your desktop and then drop it into the program of your choice to start your mood board.

Here's my approach to space planning:

Clear your room of all furniture. You want to see it as a blank slate.

Measure the length and height of each wall. Pull out your phone and record a video while you are doing this, calling out the dimensions as you go, so you have a backup for your written measurements. You want to create a visual representation, a bird's-eye view, of your room. I like to have a rudimentary sketch or floor plan of each room in my binder. Don't worry so much about its being to scale—I'm not asking you to turn into an architect—but do make sure to include the proper measurements in the plan.

Measure all the windows, including the frames, and note where the windows are in the room and the space between doors and window frames.

Consider all the variables. Make sure to factor in things like door heights and tricky hallway angles. You don't want to have to cross your fingers that the new sofa you are excited about is going to fit in the room or even through the front door. (I once had a client who lived in an apartment, and with anything over 6 feet long, we had to ask their neighbor across the hall to open their door so that we could tilt the furniture inside. No one wants that kind of drama.)

Note any existing features in the room. If there are built-ins, like a dry bar or a bookshelf, now is the time to break out that measuring tape and record their dimensions.

Painter's tape is your friend. Measure out a furniture arrangement or gallery wall on the floor before you bring items into the space or hang up art. This will give you a visual of where the furniture will sit or how a gallery wall will look. Use the least adhesive version of the tape so you don't damage the floor.

Add all these measurements to your space plan. I want you to keep in mind the height of furnishings in conjunction with the ceiling height, for example. At this stage, don't overthink the design. You are just looking to record the details of your space.

I Measured Everything. Now What?

Once you have your measurements recorded, start to visualize the flow of the space, and plot out where everything is going to live. I like tackling this stage with blue painter's tape to map out everything on the floor.

This is one of the easiest ways for people to space plan without having to learn a fancy software program.

Tape out where you want your furniture to go, then ask yourself, "Is this sofa wide enough?" "What size rug do we need?" Just because you find a great rug on sale doesn't mean it will work in your space. Without measuring for it, you might get it home and realize that you needed one size up to fill the space, or worse, that it's too big and climbing up your walls. You really don't want to guess when it comes to scale.

While you have the room cleared out, test a variety of layouts to decide on the best flow for the space. Often, you'll find you can fit in more than you think. For example, the sofa arranged one way doesn't leave room for an ottoman, but turning the sofa to face a different direction gives you space for extra seating that would have otherwise been lost. Trying different layouts will enable you to experiment and see what works and what doesn't. And more than anything, it will help you determine the correct scale.

Opposite: Pinterest is fine for early planning, but nothing compares to seeing paint and textile swatches in person to confirm they'll work in your space.

sage tint

459

woodland green

460

herb bouquet

461

rosepine

vintage vogue

1593

...ker gray

When it comes to scale, one of the most common items people need help with is the television. Before you jump on that great sale price on Black Friday, consider how the TV will match up to the space in your entertainment center or on your wall. Use that painter's tape and mark where your TV will live. Then ask yourself, "Is our TV going to look a little wimpy? Can we go larger?" Or "Is our current TV too big?" Scale is one thing you can play with at this stage, and you want to get it right before you run to the store.

Opposite: When you go thrifting, definitely let yourself fall in love with a huge anchoring piece, like this oversized china cabinet; however, keep in mind how it will fit in with the room's other pieces (the art, the furniture, and the rug). And remember to consider your ceiling height before you pull the trigger!

Making Note of Scale

You might be wondering how exactly one judges scale. A couple rules of thumb: select a rug on which at least the front two legs of the sofa or chair fit, and a coffee table that's half to two-thirds the length of the sofa.

When measuring for a large piece of furniture, like an armoire, focus less on the height at first. Think about the other dimensions and how they'll work in the space. Will the piece stick out, block a high-traffic area, or be oddly out of proportion with other pieces in the room? Once you have figured out the scale of your space, you can zero in on the perfect pieces.

When you're beginning to put your space plan together, start with your big anchoring pieces, the must-haves like your sofa, the entertainment center, a bookcase, and anything that is a permanent fixture. Then you can work around the room, moving on to your accessories.

This is also a good time to consider the scale of your light fixtures. It's important to make sure you have enough ceiling height to accommodate them or that they will fit on your wall. You don't want to end up with disproportional lights. If they're too small, it can look like you live in a dollhouse, and that's not a good thing. On the flip side, you don't want a fixture so large that it blocks other focal points in the room. This is where knowing the room dimensions is so important. Height will play an important role when you're deciding between sconces and pendant lighting. If you have 12-foot ceilings, you don't want a tiny fixture that gets lost. Instead, look for a chandelier that hangs 30 to 36 inches down and fills the space.

Graph paper will help you to scale a room. Each box can represent the space you would like it to; for example, if you have a 10-by-10-foot room, use ten boxes on the graph paper to represent each foot in the space.

Other Things to Consider

Beyond measurements, think about the natural light flowing into the room, for example, in relation to where you think large pieces of furniture might live. How will the fabric fare if you need to place the sofa near the window? Do you have to plan for a different configuration?

Check where all your electrical outlets are and if you have enough in the room. Make sure heavy pieces of furniture aren't blocking them and that they are still accessible.

Things Are Looking Up

Once you have the room's flow figured out, it's time to think about height. Height is an especially important consideration when you measure for drapes or bookshelves. When I do a space plan, I measure the windows' width, height, and depth—all these measurements will matter. I also measure all my doorframes. Along with the distance from the floor to the ceiling, these numbers will tell you exactly how much space you need for light fixtures, tall furniture, and window treatments. Putting all this information into your space plan will help you tremendously. I get out graph paper and draw my floor plan or any sketches of the space I might want to use.

Now that you have the larger anchoring pieces in place, you can begin to plan for smaller decor items like art, books, vases, and plants, as well as secondary furniture items like chairs and coffee tables.

To wrap it up, here's your main takeaway: your space plan is the foundation of your design bible. You should always have it on hand. I personally like to have a hard copy so I can write things down and make notes, when needed, directly on my plan. But save it to your phone if that works best for you. Something to keep in mind is that you will be adding to your space plan as you select paint, appliances, and other elements. This is going to set the framework for your forever home.

Opposite: Placing a vase on a pedestal is a wonderful way to add visual interest to your room while also filling a small amount of space. Keep an eye out at estate and tag sales for large clay or stone vases and urns, which can be had for a fraction of the cost of a marble bust and yet look just as regal.

ESSENTIAL
SPACE-PLANNING TOOLS

- Tape measure
- Painter's tape
- Camera phone or camera
- Three-ring binder
- Pen or pencil
- Graph paper
- Ruler
- Notepad
- Blank paper
- Plastic sleeves or folders for your three-ring binder

When you are out and about and you see a piece of furniture that you think might work in your space, pull out your camera phone, take a picture of the item, and use the camera editing and writing tools to mark up the image with the dimensions, color options, and where you found the piece. You can do the same with screenshots when you see something on social media or in a magazine. Keep all this inspiration in a folder on your phone for easy access. This will conserve your time and energy in the long run.

One benefit to creating a hard-copy design bible is that you can add clear plastic sleeves to save paint chips, appliance warranties, and anything else that you will need to keep handy for the duration of your time in the home. It will save you time to start your space planning in binder form and add to it as you change your space.

Above, right, and opposite:
When traveling or thrifting, don't overlook smaller vintage items, which can add meaningful layers to your home story. They can be stored easily until you find a place for them to be displayed, and you'll likely regret not getting them.

SET THE MOOD

Creating an
Unforgettable Ambiance

Opposite: The way the lighting hits
an object you've styled becomes
part of the mood you are setting in your
home. Look for items with lots
of texture, especially plants, which
add to the harmony of any space.

You might be wondering, Mikel, what does mood have to do with my forever home? My friend, everything! Creating a mood in your space allows you to add luxury to your home on any budget, without a large overhaul of your space, and essentially without any construction.

With each of my designs, I think about the mood it conveys. The mood is like a song evoking emotion when you hear it. I'm no scientist, but setting the right tone in your home can hit those same sweet spots in your brain. One of the most valuable skills I learned working on TV sets is how to produce theatrical moments that entice and captivate. My goal is to leave you feeling like, *Oh my gosh, I have to be here. I want to be here. I don't want to leave.*

A mood is a feeling, and generating one in your home might seem daunting, but I'm here to help. When I walk into a well-designed restaurant or hotel, I have a visceral reaction. I love the ambiance, the lighting. I find myself fully immersed in my environment. As I start to peel back my surroundings, I notice that it's the smallest sensory details—the smells, the flow, the comfort, the luxury of the design—that are working together to create that reaction. I feel surrounded by indulgence in the best way.

We go on vacation because we want to be transported away from our everyday lives. Let's take what works for these destinations and use it as a template in our own homes.

Without creating a mood in our homes, we are left with a blank white shell. The walls might shelter us, but they won't elicit joy, draw us home, or allow for elements of our personality to peek out. And the idea that you must own your home to create the sort of sanctuary you deserve is a farce. Let me repeat—we all deserve to live in a space that makes us feel at home.

When creating ambiance, think back to a place that made you feel safe or evoked memories of comfort. Or think of a time in your life to which you'd like to return. Can you re-create those sentiments through the design of your home? It might mean painting the walls a certain color or incorporating a favorite piece of furniture. Or maybe it's about the layout of a room or the inclusion of a beloved fabric. These moments of warmth or richness will ground you in your space.

Opposite: The reclaimed barn door is no longer functional but serves as a striking backdrop.
Above: Adding wooden decor and accessories are easy ways to flood a space with character.

Getting a Little Boutique Hotel Bougie

I love a beautifully laid out hotel. From the lobby to the on-site restaurant all the way up to the room, I always lean on hotel design for inspiration. And I want to help you think about ways to incorporate some of those beautiful hotel looks into your forever home.

One of the things people usually love about boutique hotels is that they hit all the right sensory notes. As soon as you step inside, you're drawn in. The lighting is on point, and the colors and wallpaper are selected with guests' experience in mind. Well-designed hotel lobbies are made to slowly carry your eyes over all the details.

Hotels have ambiance down to a science. It might be the scent in the air or the soft music playing. Whatever the case, your senses are immediately engaged.

Personally, I'm a big fan of the Four Seasons in Miami, which has a Spanish-modern feel. When you pull up, you feel like you're at a retreat in another country; everything is super clean, and there's repetition within the design. The outside is landscaped with palm trees, which lead you inside to a hallway lined with more palms.

Playing with greenery in this way is an easy thing to do in your own home. Maybe you don't want to line your hallway with palm trees, but perhaps you do want a fiddle-leaf fig, an olive tree, or even a Meyer lemon tree to repeat in your space. Or you might want to fill a corner with a group of plants in different sizes, creating a dramatic effect. Decide on what works for your home based on your natural light conditions and the plants' needs. When in doubt, you can always opt for artificial plants.

Hotels are great at creating cozy and inviting spaces. How can you achieve that same feeling in your own home, using what you already have? Maybe you just need to do some clever rearranging, or maybe it's as simple as adding velvety soft pillows to your sofa.

As you envision the hotel lobby of your dreams, think about the lighting and color in your space. Something hotels do so well, even in the daylight, is use ambient light in the ceiling to create a mood meant to instantly transport the guests. You can mimic this in your own home by applying dimmers to all your lights and/or lowering the wattage of your lightbulbs. Color can play a role in creating ambiance, too. Pulling in colors that give you the feel of water is an easy way to bring calm and a sense of welcome into a space,

Opposite: When creating a cozy room, think about more than just the furniture. Lighting goes a long way in making a space feel inviting, and here the copper accents in a dramatic chandelier and retro tripod floor lamp warm up the room's modern design.

reminiscent of a five-star seaside resort. If you prefer the look of all white, add pops of blue to transport yourself to the beach while never leaving your home. Clearing the clutter for a crisp, clean look will also elevate your space.

SMOKE AND MIRRORS

A set design 101 trick, which I learned from a mentor of mine, Kelli Bishop-Pope, involves using faux plants and greenery. People will often see a photo of a beautiful plant on social media, on a TV show, or in a magazine, and think, *Oh my goodness, I now want an olive tree.* Well, unless you live in California, where you have a Mediterranean climate, an olive tree isn't going to thrive in your house. The same rule applies to a clementine or lemon tree. It's nice outside, but the plant can't live in a pot on your console table. Enter faux plants, which, mind you, Kelli is not a fan of. Kelli served as an art director on *The Nate Berkus Show* and *The Martha Stewart Show,* so she really worked with the best! One of the most helpful rules of thumb she shared with me was that if the plant is touchable and sitting at the forefront, like on a coffee table or a sideboard, then make it real. If the plant will live in a spot that's not easily accessible, like on top of a bookshelf, in a corner of a room, or on a high shelf in the kitchen, opt for the artificial version. If you spend a little more, you can find faux plants that look incredibly real. Line the top of the "soil" with petrified moss to fill any remaining empty space.

Opposite: Go full-on drama with a large plant in the bedroom. If you have enough greenery to fill the space, you might not even need curtains.

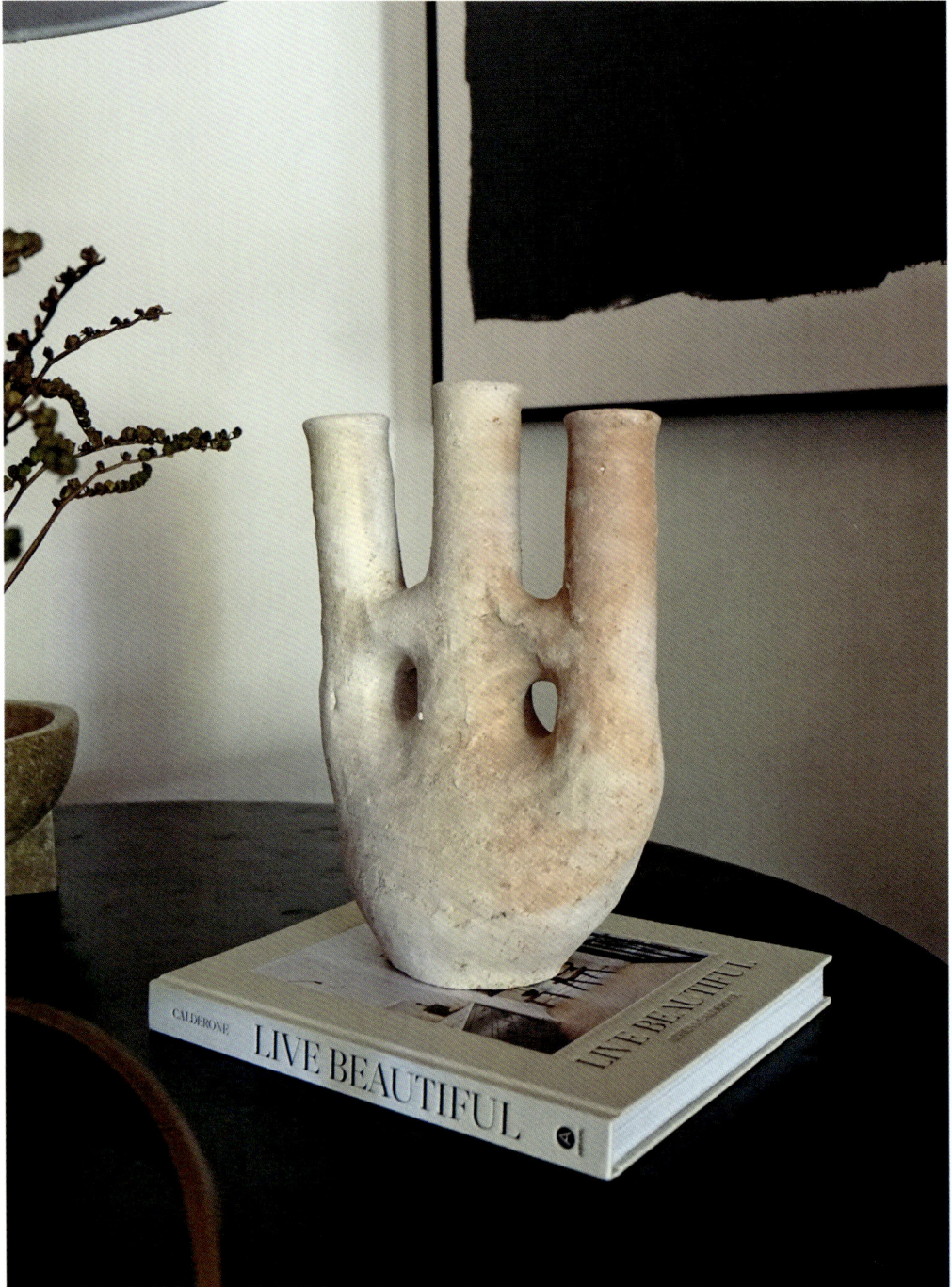

Above and opposite: You don't need to collect a lot of items to communicate your tastes. A beloved object sitting on a beautiful book or an interesting mirror with a row of candles can go a long way.

Let's All Line Up

Symmetry provides balance in our home design. Think about how you arrange the items on your bookshelves or the glassware on your open shelves in the kitchen. If you add a lush drapery treatment on either side of your entryway, you are drawing the eyes to where you want them to look. You are making the symmetry work for you without trying.

When directing the focus in a room, think about what you are centering the room around. Is it a fireplace? Windows? Shelves? I want you to ask yourself, "How can repetition and symmetry work in my favor within my home?" This is the cornerstone of creating mood and ambiance while borrowing inspiration from your favorite hotels.

Also, let's try to move away from allowing word associations and stores to dictate what an item should be used for. Get creative, think outside the box, and find your own use for your multiuse finds.

If you seek a moody vibe, look for wallpaper that transports you to a rainy day in Vermont with subtle patterns and darker colors. If wallpaper is not in the plan, opt for a dark, rich paint color. Add ambient light and you are suddenly transported to the Cotswolds, with a cozy vibe perfect for a bedroom that makes you want to crawl into bed with a book.

SMOKE AND MIRRORS

I love a beautiful pedestal. I might use it in a dining room to hold a vessel of cut branches or a piece of sculptural decor. Often, the pedestals I gravitate toward are $700 to $800. No, thank you, at that price. I head to the garden center, and for around $100, I find a beautiful resin planter, turn it upside down, and voilà—a pedestal. It has a drainage hole in the bottom, but you will have that covered, and no one will be the wiser. You can also look for a planter with a lovely patina, giving you a warmer look.

FIVE HOTELS WITH DESIGNS TO INSPIRE YOU IN YOUR OWN HOME

- Four Seasons Hotel Miami
  (Florida)
- Soho Farmhouse
  (Oxfordshire, United Kingdom)
- The Double Red Duke
  (Clanfield, United Kingdom)
- The Hoxton
  (locations throughout the world)
- The Ned Hotel
  (New York City, New York)
- Palihouse
  (locations throughout the United States)

Above, right, and opposite: From the fabric you select for the furniture and pillows to the airiness of the curtains you hang, choose materials that will allow your space to transport you and leave you living in simple luxury.

Re-creating Hotel Bathrooms at Home

When you want a hotel-style bathroom in your home, base the room around the bathtub. If a claw-foot tub is in your budget, splurge on it. If space allows for a shower only, invest in beautiful, high-quality faucets. This is an easy change you can make to upgrade the design very quickly and within any budget, whether you rent or own your home. The goal is to create a spa-like feel.

SMOKE AND MIRRORS

Wherever you love to vacation, bring a part of that hotel stay home. For example, consider finding the shampoo they offer or bedding that reminds you of the hotel. Nobody ever wants to end their vacation, so you will be extending yours in your home.

Opposite: Leave room in your budget for good-quality faucets and handles, especially if you aren't changing out the sink, tub, or shower. An upgrade in hardware can elevate your space for a fraction of the cost of replacing the entire fixture, and because these pieces are also functional, you'll be glad you made the investment in the long run.

Above and opposite: Tile is a fun item to splurge on, but if you're not planning a total renovation, invest in luxury bath products and towels, which will trick you and your guests into having that getaway state of mind.

SMOKE AND MIRRORS

We often forget about the importance of smell, but think about a vacation and seek out scents that transport you to a favorite place. Many hotels pump a selective scent through the air vents. It's calculated and meant to be part of the experience. Elevate your home in the same way. Maybe it's through a certain flower that grows in the area you are trying to emulate. Look for a candle or a room spray that uses that flower as the base of its fragrance.

As you re-create looks from your
favorite restaurants at home,
use these questions as a guide.

- How does the banquette in a
  restaurant make you feel? If it
  evokes a memory of a place
  you loved, think about opting for
  a banquette instead of a typical
  dining setup.
- Does the tufting of a booth evoke
  your favorite restaurant? Consider
  bringing that style into your living
  room with a Chesterfield sofa.
- Are you drawn to neutrals but love
  the pops of color in a favorite
  restaurant? Try bringing in color in
  a low-commitment way through
  pillows or throws.
- Could you paint the ceiling or tile
  the floor in a kitchen or bathroom
  in a colorway that is reminiscent of
  one you admire in a restaurant but
  that also feels authentic to you?
  Maybe incorporate a herringbone
  or striped pattern in a variety of
  colors that tie the elements of the
  room together in a subtle way?
- What art could you add to the space?
  Bold art is another way to bring
  pops of color into your home without
  leaving your comfort zone.

I'll Take Your Restaurant Design to Go, Please

Design-driven restaurants, like boutique hotels, are known for creating an emotional and sensory experience. Restaurants are in the business of telling a story and transporting you. They have already done the work, pushed the boundaries, tested things out, and found what works. How you take their design cues and work them into your home is up to you, but to get you started, consider how the art on the walls relates to the furniture, in both the color of the fabric and the warmth of the frame or the texture and colors within the art itself. Notice how a certain light fixture might work in your own space with your chosen dining room table. Maybe you'd like to place floor-to-ceiling bookshelves in the dining room to add warmth and character. Think about your favorite restaurant's dishware, flatware, and glassware; how could you use those selections as inspiration in your forever home? You want the space you are creating to transport you to a place and time that left a lasting impression on you.

Opposite: Think back to a favorite
restaurant experience and look for ways
to incorporate its design elements to
echo the memory. Start by acquiring
similar dishware and table linens and
build from there.

Turn on the table lamp, cut the
overhead lighting, and create ambiance
in your space. I love using wall sconces
to lend both calm and intimacy while
also illuminating the artwork.

Why Lighting Matters

Think back to the most theatrical lighting you have ever seen in a
restaurant.

How did it make you feel?

Restaurants are the risk-takers; we are the note-takers.

Learn from what restaurants do well and apply their choices
to your own home. Lighting influences all of us, even if we don't
realize it. The fluorescent lighting in an office setting has a much
different feel than the dim, cozy lighting in a restaurant or hotel.
When creating an over-the-top lighting experience, consider using
a chandelier that features a cluster of three or four globes and keeping the rest of the room simple. A beautiful crystal chandelier can
sometimes feel excessive and too ornate, but when it's paired with
neutral furnishings, then the overpowering look is muted. Mix
dramatic lighting with symmetry in your furniture, and you've
unlocked a heavenly thing, a designer's secret.

Opposite: If you come across a big
dramatic piece of lighting you love,
try to find a place for it in your home.
It will catch the eye of everyone who
walks through the door.

If you aren't ready to live with drama in an entire room, think about creating a theatrical moment in the entryway with an antique door or maybe a hand-carved door from India or Mexico.

Another place to add drama is around your bed. I like to take simple drapery rods and, instead of draping the windows, drape the bed. This effect resembles what you might have seen in Marie Antoinette's bedchamber. Keep it neutral—it doesn't have to be ostentatious. You could also hang a muted and understated panel of drapery at the end of the bed or behind the headboard, place a bench made of found driftwood at the foot of your bed, or turn an art panel or antique door into a headboard.

On Finding the Theatrical Design Moments

With set design, I need some drama and something that's going to catch your eye, and even somebody like me who loves beige and oatmeal has to use a little color to make people engage with and want to be in a space. When I'm looking for these moments, these ways to add drama, I want to make sure I'm also telling a story with my designs.

What do you want your room to say to anyone who enters it? Incorporate your story into your design. Say your child or partner loves sports—create a gallery wall featuring their trophies and medals on small wall pedestals and in shadow boxes, mixed with vintage black-and-white photographs of the sport of choice. The story is there, presented in a way that's classy and in line with the rest of the home.

I once decorated a penthouse apartment where, when you opened the door, you were greeted by a 12-foot-long bench under dramatic, moody lighting. The bench was so long that it had to ride up on top of the elevator car!

Embrace this type of theatrical moment. Think about using large plants or trees in surprising ways. An oversized tree would typically sit on the floor, but why not place one on a console table? I am notorious for putting large plants in unusual places, which creates drama and draws the eyes upward. When you have a room with high ceilings, this is an especially nice touch because you want to not only draw the eyes upward but also give them a place to land. Theatrical moments are those unexpected details that give your home a wow factor.

Who says gold finishes need to be only on the hardware of the fixtures? Get instant glamour with gold-leaf wallpaper.

SMOKE AND MIRRORS

You don't need to break the bank to have a little fun and splurge on opulent details. Small spaces like a powder room or a walk-in closet are where you can take a few chances without stretching your budget too far. Hang a petite chandelier in the closet, or install gold-leaf wallpaper in the powder room. But don't stop there—gold-leaf the ceiling, too. Is it a little over-the-top? Maybe, but it's also a statement. And you can always close the door!

**IMPERFECT ITEMS TO
LOOK FOR**

- Concrete and plaster vases
- Old books
- Worn textiles
- Small sculptures
- Glassware
- Silverware
- Pottery
- Planters
- Wood vessels or bowls
- Vintage artwork

**PLACES TO LOOK FOR
IMPERFECT PIECES**

- Flea markets
- Thrift shops
- Local online marketplaces
- Pawnshops
- Vintage stores, online and in-person
- eBay
- Etsy

Filling the Walls with Art

Everyone's favorite theatrical moment: the gallery wall! It's even more dramatic when you take the artwork all the way up to the ceiling. With a gallery wall, you can have some fun with your design and incorporate a bunch of personalities. This is your chance to play with a variety of frames and canvases. The lighting of the gallery wall will contribute to making it a showstopper in your home.

Embracing the Imperfect

I'm someone who loves vintage and thrifted items. I think a big part of creating ambiance is finding pieces that have character; everything doesn't have to be pristine. I also love pieces made of natural elements like wood, stone, and plaster, things that already have a patina to them or are going to weather over time. Sure, they might become chipped or stained, but they give a room soul. The great thing about items that might read as imperfect is that they tell a story even when you might not have one, and they often look like heirlooms. They can enrich your space, so don't be afraid to embrace the imperfect.

SMOKE AND MIRRORS

If your room is lacking in architectural detail, don't be afraid to add some—maybe wood beams on the ceiling or wainscoting on the walls. I've even used foam to create faux wood beams; this cuts down on costs and weight while still adding a design element that elevates the room. Consider getting an estimate from a contractor or designer to bring more character to your home; ask about adding crown molding or door trim. Turn to sites like Pinterest to discover details you are drawn to that would also work with the era of your home.

Opposite: When you have a room where only a large piece of art will do, think outside the box. An art piece doesn't always have to be framed, nor does it even have to be a traditional painting or print. In this room, we used a tapestry featuring a fanciful design, which tied into the surrounding walls and artwork.

Creating a beautiful space is like making art. When an artist creates a painting, for example, they might know they want to use black, white, and gray but not know how the piece is going to come out. So they experiment until it makes sense. Approach design in the same way. Move things around and swap items in and out until the arrangement makes sense for you, your design, and your space.

Toss in the Unexpected

When creating ambiance, you want some elements people wouldn't naturally incorporate or gravitate toward; maybe even some that are a little controversial. Not everyone is going to love everything, and that's fine. It's about what you love and what makes you happy. This is your forever home. Maybe you love the look of a monochromatic bookshelf. It's rather frowned upon, but I've been known to take the covers off books to expose the spines, favoring the raw look of the white or cream pages. I'll use dollar-store books and fill the shelves with the coverless books. It's a very theatrical moment, which is also very inexpensive to create. Go a step further and hang a piece of artwork at the center of the shelves. Again, very unexpected, but this is for you. Make the mood yours.

SMOKE AND MIRRORS

We live in a time when the classic board-and-batten look is ruling the home. This timeless look can easily be achieved with a simple DIY project. You can use this treatment in dining rooms, bathrooms, hallways, and bedrooms. Head to the hardware store and pick up 1-inch-thick wood boards in lengths based on the design you want to create. You just level the boards and nail them to the wall, then either paint them to match the wall or stain the wood. Or try using a peel-and-stick picture frame molding kit for a similar effect. This is a different feature than board-and-batten, but each will give you a new architectural vibe in your forever home.

Opposite: When creating drama, allow yourself to consider how vintage and box-store vases can be arranged together. You don't have to spend a lot to create a look that is warm and inviting, and if styled just right, the mix will elevate your space.

ADD UNEXPECTED DESIGN ELEMENTS TO YOUR FOREVER HOME

- Create barn doors for an area you want to hide.
- Place a large plant or small tree beside a sofa to create a sense of drama.
- Hang a piece of art off-center on a wall, then balance it with a large tree for a double dose of the unexpected in your design.
- Bring a showstopper to your bathroom by way of a copper or claw-foot bathtub.
- Mix finishes, like matte black fixtures, with your new copper tub.
- Opt for a hanging daybed instead of a sofa.
- Use tiles in the same pattern but different colors on the floor and walls of a bathroom for a fun mix of texture and pattern.

Right and opposite: Using natural elements in your home that will last a long time is a fun way to bring the outdoors in. Moss is a design option few people consider using. And think about the placement of a plant—in this case a tree. If the height of the ceiling allows for it, raise the plant to direct the eye upward.

FIND COLOR BALANCE

After graduating from Morehouse College in Atlanta, I moved back to my parents' home in Detroit to save money and figure out my next steps. My childhood bedroom was clad in white, and it just wasn't working for the aesthetic I'd discovered I was drawn to. So I decided to paint the walls a dark and moody chocolate brown. Then I went to Crate & Barrel and purchased some items from the sale section to pull the look together. My mother was nervous the whole time. She was afraid the room would be dark and claustrophobic. I didn't listen to her, however, and the color scheme of brown, beige, and cream (I know, not a shocker) ended up turning out exactly as I'd envisioned. Both of my parents were impressed. All that to say, I've been pushing the boundaries with color for a long time and have a history of doing the unpredictable. I want you to walk away from this chapter with the courage to experiment with colors. At the end of the day, you can always repaint walls. Painting is the most forgiving part of home design, so jump in, take a little risk, and push the color wheel with hues you wouldn't normally pick.

Opposite: Color is a design element on which you can base everything else. It brings a room together, even a neutral hue like this. Remember to think about how objects in the room work with the color selections. Here, we layered in lots of white accessories to offset the dark wood and upholstery.

When you embrace the monochromatic look, you have to go all in, painting the doors, the trim, the baseboards—everything—the same color as the walls. If you don't, you will be left with trim that sticks out in an otherwise calm room.

All in One Hue: Monochromatic Rooms

One of the most timeless color trends, with good reason, is using just one tone on the crown molding, walls, trim, doors, baseboards and ceiling. A monochromatic room makes all the details look super clean and gives your eyes a place to rest. Another benefit to the monochromatic approach is that you don't have to worry about coordinating paint colors with each other. (But when you are setting up your forever home, the color of the paint might dictate whether you need to restain your floors.)

When you decide to paint the entire room one color, you are allowing the furniture and art in the space to shine, to be the star. This approach sets the framework for you to introduce any other colors you want to bring into the space through accessories. For an added fun feature, take an old piece of wood furniture—such as a small desk in a bedroom or a bookshelf in the living room—that needs to be repainted or stained and paint it the same color as the walls. Let it blend in, and add contrasting pops of color with things like plants and books.

Opposite: If you're typically color shy, consider matching the molding to the baseboards for a monochromatic look. For sure it's a commitment, but the effect will be timeless.

Finding Your True Colors

When working on a set, I must quickly change color schemes to complement the design I'm creating. Furniture moves around, fabrics get swapped out, and the backdrop needs to follow suit. I have my go-to colors handy, so I already know my options and can build the design from there. Well, because I want your house to be the best it can be and I know how hard it is to make color selections, I'm sharing my secrets with you.

I put together ten sets of colors that work well together. I will walk you through finding the tones that work best for you and applying those colors to your space.

Each set of three colors is based on my tried-and-true groupings.

- The largest of the three circles is your wall color. This will be what you base everything else in the room around.

- The medium circle represents the primary piece of furniture; for the bedroom, that would be your bed, for the living room, your sofa, and so on.

- The smaller dot is for accessories to include in the space.

Look for ways to incorporate different groupings into your home, room by room, for continuity and calm throughout. You can adjust by tone; for example, if you land on a light blue, find the tone of blue you are most drawn to.

When you are first deciding on a color, don't feel the need to rush. Use peel-and-stick paint samples or paint onto a nice piece of linen paper that you tape to the wall, and give it a little time. See how the light from the windows streams in at different times of day and impacts the appearance of the paint sample on the wall. Look at how lamplight works with the colors on rainy days and in the evening. You are allowed not to commit until you see what works best for you.

Opposite: If you're drawn to white walls and neutral furnishings, you can introduce pops of color through pillows and other accessories. That way, you can switch out the color whenever you want.

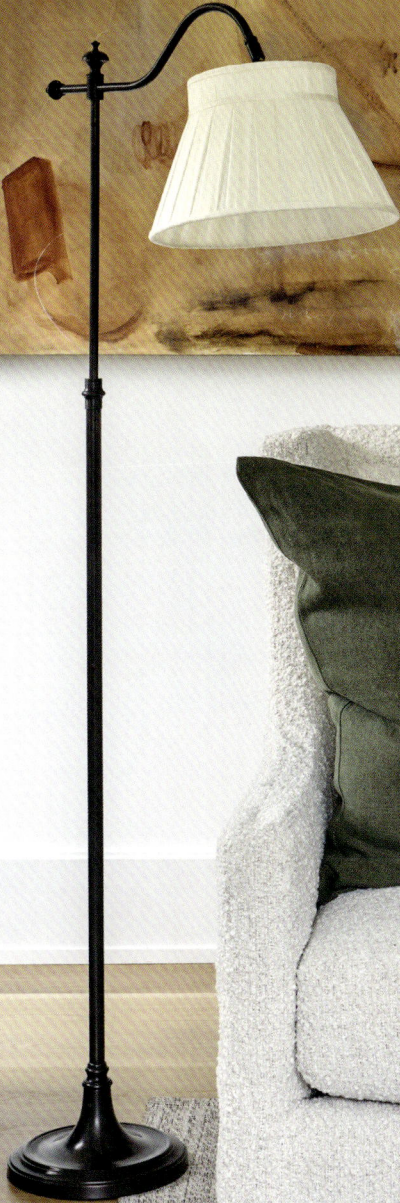

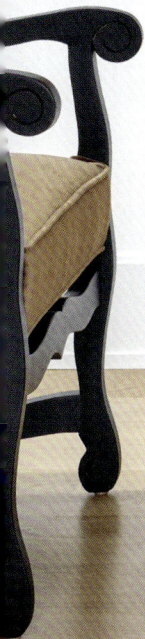

Dark and Moody Color Groupings

Forest green
Chocolate brown
Off-white or beige

Navy blue
Creamy off-white
Blue gray

Smoky gray
Tan or beige
Copper

Black
White or off-white
Dark brown

Plum
Rose
Cream

Ochre
Off-white
Tan

Above and on page 93: When choosing artwork, keep in mind the colors and the style of the room in which you want to hang it. It should be a piece that you love but also one that speaks to your overall design.

Warm and Bright Color Groupings

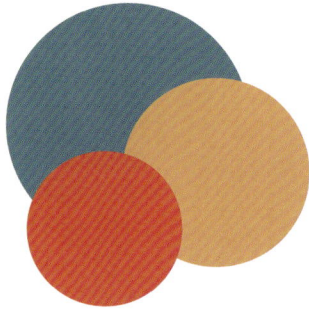

Medium-tone blue
Khaki or goldenrod
Salmon

Sage green
Light blue
Ochre

Mauve
Dark cyan
Stone

Blush pink
Muted purple
Cream

Terra-cotta
Off-white
Beige

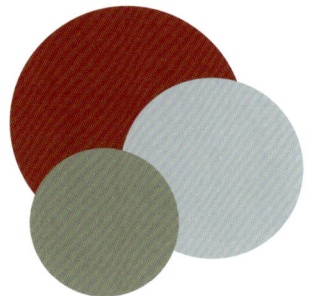

Wine red
Light blue
Sage green

When I'm trying to find colors that work together, I often turn to fashion for inspiration. I look at how the colors of the fabrics work together and how I can apply them to a room design. Make a mood board if you are a visual person like me. Draw out a floor plan and attach your paint samples to the drawing to see how the colors flow from one room to the next. Hang paint samples together on the wall to see how they feel next to one another.

Opposite: A dark and moody bedroom creates a space where sleep rules the roost. Darker colors can ground a room in a much different way than their lighter and airy counterparts.

Welcome to the Dark Side

If you have found yourself being scared of darker colors or asking yourself, "Is the room going to be too dark?" or "Will it make the room feel smaller?," then buckle up because I'm going to hold your hand through this process and help you transition to the dark side.

First things first, we aren't magicians—paint or no paint, we can't make a room smaller. Paint, however, does have the power to make a room feel cozy, and coziness is something every home needs. I want to show you how you can have a dark room that's inviting, while also creating an optical illusion to make your space feel larger. If you are afraid of color, you can use the dark color you are drawn to paired with a complementary lighter tone to balance things out and make you more comfortable with this new look. And there are also other ways to use darker tones. You can paint the walls in a dark color and paint the baseboards and doors in a lighter tone, such as white or cream; or you can flip that idea and paint the trim of a light room in a dark tone, like navy blue or dark green.

Dark colors make your space feel grounded, and in bedrooms, deep tones can help you fall asleep.

When you decide to go dark, I suggest opting for a matte finish (more on paint sheens in the following pages). If the paint is too reflective and not subdued, trust me, it just won't work the way you hope it will.

When darker tones are applied correctly, you will always get that feeling of warmth and coziness; the feeling of autumn that everybody loves will envelop you. Earth tones contribute to a sense of calm. I'm naturally drawn to these tones when designing a space because they're timeless and classic, richer and darker—in other words, they're forever home tones. You don't have to keep the walls white. In fact, I encourage you not to.

SMOKE AND MIRRORS

When I worked on the show *Pickler & Ben*, guests would enter through these large, classic iron doors. Only, guess what? They were made of wood. We clad the wood door with hardware meant for doors primarily used outside, and painted everything a rich, dark black. This is a great way to give your home an industrial look without spending a lot of money. If you are building a house or just looking for a refresh, you could apply this smoke and mirrors treatment to your window casings and doors for a classic faux-iron-finish look.

Many paint stores can upload a picture of your room to their computer and create a visual for you to see what the specific shade will look like before you commit. If this service is offered in your area, honey, use it. It's fantastic for helping you decide on a color.

Finding the Right Paint Sheen

Many people don't really understand which paint sheen (also called a paint finish) is best to use in each space in their home. Fortunately, you have your designer right here in your hands, and I'm happy to break it down for you.

Flat

A flat sheen is not reflective, so it provides a perfect backdrop in areas where you don't want any shine, and is also great for hiding imperfections. For example, it's not going to draw as much attention to paint drips or a spot that wasn't properly sanded. If you are interested in trying out a flat sheen paint, the ceiling is a great place to start. A flat finish is ideal for the person who does not touch the walls and treats their house like it's in a magazine spread. At all times.

- **Nonreflective:** Flat paint is ideal for areas where you don't want a shiny look.
- **Conceals imperfections:** Although flat paint is the best finish for hiding imperfections on surfaces, it's the least resistant to stains.
- **Suitable for:** Ceilings, living rooms, bedrooms, and spaces where wear and tear or messy splatters are not major concerns.

Opposite: Flat sheen paint used in a low-traffic area of a home is ideal for rooms you don't use as often, such as a guest bedroom or powder room.

- Lay out the paper on the floor to protect your floors.
- Clean any vents that are in the room.
- Take a full day just to prep the walls: patch and repair any cracks, properly sand any bumps, and make sure the walls are super clean.
- Tape off all the walls and windows.
- Remove all the covers for your electrical outlets and light switches.

When protecting floors before you start painting, put tape around the baseboards and a thick layer of caulk over the tape so that paint doesn't seep underneath.

Opposite: A matte paint finish works well for deeply saturated tones, giving them a more elegant feel. It's also more forgiving to fingerprints and smudges.

Matte

Just one step up from a flat sheen is matte paint. It has a very low-luster effect, a subtle shine. On many of my projects, I use a matte finish. Like flat paint, it's going to hide the imperfections on surfaces, but a matte finish will be a little more forgiving with stains than a flat one. So if you do splash something on the wall, you can wipe it off without worrying about the paint color going away completely. This sheen is perfect for families with kids or pets.

- **Low luster:** Matte paint provides a subtle shine, slightly more than flat paint but less than other finishes.

- **Conceals imperfections:** Like a flat finish, a matte sheen helps conceal imperfections on the surface, but it performs better than flat paint in terms of stain resistance.

- **Suitable for:** Ceilings, living rooms, bedrooms, and areas where you want a non-glossy finish without worrying about stains or damage.

Eggshell

The middle-of-the-road, safe choice of sheen is eggshell. It has a slightly glossy look as well as an elegant feel. The best part about eggshell is you can wipe it down with a wet cloth and not have to worry about the paint rubbing off; it really sticks to the walls. Unlike flat or matte finishes, an eggshell sheen is forgiving. Before you begin to paint, your walls need to be in good shape and prepped properly. Do any sanding that needs to be done, or if you have any cracks in the wall, go ahead and fill those before you paint because otherwise you will have issues later.

- **Slightly shiny:** A step up from flat or matte paint, eggshell paint has a slight sheen, providing a more elegant finish.

- **Easy to clean:** Eggshell paint is easier to clean than flat or matte paint.

- **Requires surface prep:** This sheen accentuates surface imperfections, so proper preparation, including scraping away cracked paint and smoothing the walls, is crucial.

Satin

This is when we start to turn the conversation toward shiny walls. With its subtle gloss, satin is one step up from eggshell, without being completely over-the-top shiny. A satin sheen is a good choice for a high-traffic family room, a well-loved living room, bedrooms, a hallway, or a busy kitchen. It's also great in kids' bedrooms since you can wipe the walls without damaging the paint. It also works well for baseboards and crown molding.

- **Slightly shinier than eggshell:** Satin offers a subtle gloss without being overly reflective.

- **Versatile:** Suitable for family rooms, living rooms, bedrooms, hallways, kitchens, dining areas, children's bedrooms, and bathrooms, and tough enough for trim.

- **Requires surface prep:** Like eggshell, satin accentuates imperfections, so it's important to prep the walls by removing bumps and peeling paint.

Semigloss

A semigloss sheen will give you a shiny and slick look. It is the toughest finish in terms of resistance to stains, and is very forgiving. You can wipe the surface, and it'll take all the wear and tear. A sheen like semigloss is also a good choice for your trim, baseboards, windows, doors, and furniture, too.

- **Shiny:** Semigloss finishes catch the light, giving your walls a vibrant look.

- **Tough and stain-resistant:** Least likely to show wear and tear, semigloss paints also stain less easily than other finishes and are easy to clean.

- **Suitable for:** Trim, windows, doors, and spaces where a shiny look is desired, such as a kid's room, kitchen, or bathrooms.

When my dad was in his twenties, he painted the house next door to my maternal grandparents'. The neighbor introduced him to my mom, so that's how they met—through paint.

If I'm painting anything in a rich tone, like navy, green, or black, I always use a gray primer instead of a white primer because the paint will go on the wall much more evenly.

Using the Right Tools Can Go a Long Way

Investing in your tools will pay off, I promise. If you get a cheap paintbrush, you will end up removing the bristles out of the wet paint on the walls, and the next thing you know, your wall will be covered in fingerprints (not to mention your fingers covered in paint). It starts a whole domino effect of issues. Do you have time for that? I don't, so I always splurge on the good paintbrushes.

The same goes for good paint rollers, which hold more paint each time you reapply it. Your time is valuable, and having good tools saves you from making extra trips to the paint tray, prolonging the job.

My father, a former housepainter, taught me to always start with the most annoying things: the crown molding, the tops and corners of the walls, and the baseboards, all of which you need to paint with a brush rather than a roller. With the walls, my rule of thumb is to paint in each corner with a brush at least 6 inches out; this allows the roller to do the rest.

Once you start to apply paint to a wall with a roller, instead of just going straight up and down, you want to draw the paint out by making either the letter M or the letter W. And I'm not saying that because I'm Mikel Welch, and those are my initials—that's the way my dad taught me. You paint an uppercase M or W very large across the wall. Then you fill in the areas where you see paint didn't go, the spaces between the vertical strokes of the M or the W, by moving the roller straight up and down or from side to side to evenly distribute the paint across the entire wall. That's how you get a perfect wall, according to a former housepainter.

SMOKE AND MIRRORS

I'm constantly using spray paint in set design. Spray paint is king. A can of paint can transform just about anything you find for free or at a thrift shop into a brand-new piece. I might find an item I love except for the color. I force myself to look past the lime green and imagine painting it a matte black. A change like that can elevate a piece very quickly. Another fun thing about spray paint is that if you go to a paint store, they can often turn any of their colors into spray paint. You might have to pay a little more, but it's worth it for the custom color selection rather than off-the-shelf options.

Once the paint is dry, you can remove the painter's tape, which is honestly one of the most satisfying parts of the entire process. When you're pulling the tape off, you want to pull it up at a 90-degree angle. Go slowly because otherwise you risk ripping the paint off the wall.

Many of my designs center neutrals, but you can embrace color if it's for you and muted tones aren't your thing. It's okay to change your design style over time; moods and tastes change, and we want some diversity in our homes as well. It's completely normal to want to try new things. That's the beauty of paint, and we can see the correlation between paint color and how our style evolves.

I think about when I was a kid. We must have repainted our bathroom three or four times. My mom was really into sponge painting in the mid-nineties. We lived with a sponge-painted bathroom for several years, and when the look felt dated, we repainted. It was a simple fix. Don't overthink paint. It's okay to explore with color in a contained environment. Leave the hallway and open-concept areas more neutral with whites and creams and save bold colors for smaller spaces where the door can be closed so the bold color or wallpaper is not so in-your-face all the time.

SMOKE AND MIRRORS

If you are planning to add wallpaper to one of your walls, a general rule of thumb is to paint the wall with a one-inch border the same color as the neighboring wall. When you stop the paint right at the edge, you're left with a line of the paint standing out rather than blending in, highlighting the imperfections. The paint won't line up properly with the wallpaper like you want it to. Painting a little of the wall ensures that you don't have any gaps.

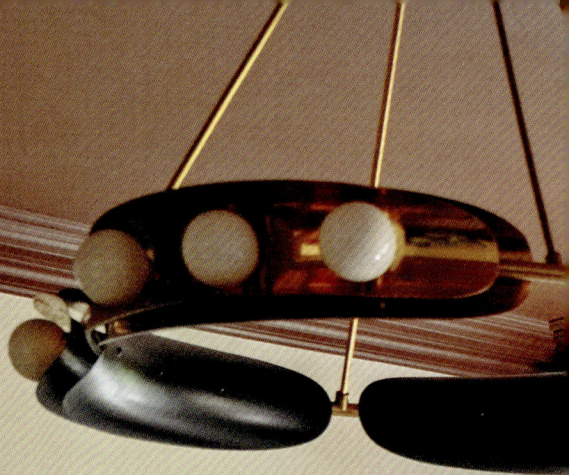

BLACKS

Starless Sky Glidden	**Cambridge** Pratt & Lambert	**Bedrock** Pratt & Lambert	**Paean Black** Farrow & Ball	**Pepper Sam** Portola Paints	**Railings** Farrow & Ball
Beetle Black Farrow & Ball	**Tricorn Black** Sherwin-Williams	**Grate Black** Farrow & Ball	**Soot** Benjamin Moore	**Blackboard** Magnolia Home	**Broadway** Behr

BLUES

Abysse Ressource	**Smokestack Gray** Benjamin Moore	**Good Jeans** Clare	**Goodnight Moon** Clare	**Hale Navy** Benjamin Moore	**Wellfleet** Portola Paints
Light Farrow & Ball	**De Nimes** Farrow & Ball	**Rainy Days** Magnolia Home	**Port Blue** Prestige	**Dark & Stormy** Dunn-Edwards	**Mirror Mirror** PPG Paints

BROWNS

Dark Ash Glidden	**Coffee Date** Clare	**Dirty Chai** Clare	**Mole's Breath** Farrow & Ball	**French Beige** Portola Paints	**Drawing Room** Magnolia Home
Deep Reddish Brown Farrow & Ball	**Black Fox** Sherwin-Williams	**Silhouette** Benjamin Moore	**Kingsport Gray** Benjamin Moore	**Fired Earth** Valspar	**Mink Brown** Dutch Boy

GRAYS

Sentimental Reasons Backdrop	**Agreeable Gray** Sherwin-Williams	**Chic Gray** Behr	**Creamy Mushroom** Behr	**Starless Sky** Glidden	**Interior Motives** Backdrop
Silver Lake Dad Backdrop	**Abalone** Benjamin Moore	**Ammonite** Farrow & Ball	**Washi** Portola Paints	**Narrows** Portola Paints	**Cornforth White** Farrow & Ball

WHITES

Pointing Farrow & Ball	**Alabaster** Sherwin-Williams	**School House White** Farrow & Ball
Snowbound Sherwin-Williams	**Decorations White** Sherwin-Williams	**Pure White** Sherwin-Williams

Swiss Coffee Benjamin Moore	**Morning Ritual** Backdrop	**Timeless** Clare
On Point Portola Paints	**Blondie** Portola Paints	**Piano Room** Portola Paints

GREENS

Dakota Shadow Benjamin Moore	**Rolling Hills** Benjamin Moore	**Mellow Mood** Clare
Current Mood Clare	**Kismet** Backdrop	**Rooted in Comfort** Dutch Boy

Highland Portola Paints	**Locally Grown** Magnolia Home	**Dark as Night** PPG Paints
Greenland Dunn-Edwards	**Pigeon** Farrow & Ball	**Stonecraft** Dunn-Edwards

Paint Like a Pro: Faux Limewash Technique

Don't be afraid to try new paint techniques, or anything else that might give you pause. Remember, painting is the most forgiving change you will make in creating your forever home.

Limewashing is one technique I truly love. It presents your walls in a very matte sheen, creating almost a velvet-like, chalky effect. I'm not trying to make this a DIY book, but this method is too good not to share.

Before you get started, make sure you have all the tools you will need to create these rich tones and soft textures.

TOOLS

- Painter's tape
- Primer (optional)
- Primary and secondary paint colors in a matte finish
- One wide paintbrush or stain brush (5 inches or wider)
- Several smaller paintbrushes
- Two small paint trays
- Small bucket

When selecting your paint colors, aim for two shades, with one being a few shades darker than the other. When you decide on a color from a sample card at your hardware store, just move up and down on the card to select another color for a stable contrast.

Opposite: I love a successful DIY design moment. When applied correctly, this limewash finish looks like velvet, leaving the room feeling luxurious for a fraction of the cost of expensive wallpaper.

Step 1: Prepare Your Canvas

Start with clean walls by wiping away any dirt or debris with a damp cloth. Consider priming the walls if you're going for a lighter-toned limewash or if the walls need extra attention. Don't forget to tape around the floor and any fixtures.

Step 2: If You're Going for a Monochromatic Look, Paint the Crown Molding, Trim, Doors, and Baseboards

Paint the molding, trim, doors, and baseboards with a couple coats of the primary paint color. A slightly darker shade in an eggshell finish can add depth.

Step 3: Apply the Limewash

Fill each paint tray with one of your two paint colors. Fill your small bucket with water. Dip the wide brush lightly into the water, then into both colors of paint, ensuring that the brush is not overloaded with paint. Starting in the middle of the wall, apply the paint with broad, random strokes. Blend the lighter and darker tones together smoothly. If the paint becomes too thick, spread it out evenly.

Step 4: Add the Finishing Touches

For an aged look, lightly drag the dry brush in vertical and horizontal strokes. Let the faux limewash dry completely before adding another layer.

SMOKE AND MIRRORS

To create a custom paint color for your home, mix two shades from the same paint strip. Make sure to note which colors you mixed and in what ratio in case you need to buy and mix more paint for touch-ups. Add the info to your design bible for quick reference as needed.

Opposite: A custom paint job elevates a room in a way that selecting a color from a paint swatch can't. From applying faux finishes to pairing two paint colors to create a custom effect, there are myriad ways to make a room your own.

Interiors   Atelier AM

THE INTERIORS OF CHESTER JONES   MERRELL

Clarke   African Art in the Barnes Foundation

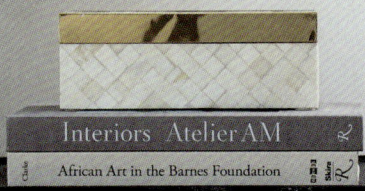

EMPHASIZE
THE
DETAILS

Renters most likely won't be selecting flooring unless it needs replacing and your landlord doesn't mind your taking the lead. Honestly, this type of landlord is a dream. However, I suggest not making a change like this without negotiating a rent discount, and making it only if you plan to be there a long time.

Choosing all the design elements of your forever home is so much fun, yet it can be overwhelming if you don't know where to start. The details are what your eyes see first when you enter your home and the items that ground your home the most. It might seem wild to worry so much about how your curtains hang or what drawer-pull length you pick, but I promise it all ties together, and you and your home will be much happier if you focus on getting these things right.

Even in a rental, there are easy ways to make the items work for you. I'll be your best friend in your ear saying, "Pick that. Don't get that." I want you to feel like I'm right there with you through all these selections, as I walk you through the process and help you make decisions on everything from flooring, rugs, and hardware to window treatments and fabrics. We will also look at how the details apply to kitchens and bathrooms.

Floors and Rugs: How to Make the Right Selections

Selecting flooring hasn't always been smooth sailing for me. Learn from my mistakes. When I was designing Steve Harvey's office, I had new flooring installed in the summer, and then suddenly, the boards started to shrink. It was a nightmare. If I had let the flooring sit for a few days, I would have given them time to expand or contract, depending on the environment.

Opposite: When selecting a rug, think about the style of your existing decor and vice versa. Marrying textures, patterns, and finishes to bring out the colors in your rug will help tie the room together.

SMOKE AND MIRRORS

People these days love to find old houses, strip the wood floors, and stain them again because the quality is there. There's nothing like a real hardwood floor, but engineered wood flooring is great, too, especially if you're trying to save money. And both can be sanded and refinished.

Decoding Flooring Types

If you are entering into a full remodel and replacing the floors, deciding among the various types of flooring can be intimidating. Let's talk about all the choices.

Hardwood

Hardwood flooring is a common and beautiful choice, with many pros and few cons. It can be sanded, refinished, and stained, which is nice because you can customize your flooring. If you are replacing the flooring, you can also decide what type of wood you would like to use—there are many options. In my opinion, hardwood floors have the most appeal overall because the material feels the most natural. If you're someone who likes character and patina, and you want a sturdy material, opt for hardwood. If you maintain your floors well, they can last for years to come.

On the negative side, obviously, hardwood floors cost a lot more than engineered wood floors. And because hardwood is a natural product that hasn't been touched, any little imperfection will be visible. Each ding is going to show up, and general wear will be more evident. So keep that in mind if you think you'll be bothered by it.

FLOORING PRICE POINTS

- Hardwood—$5 to $10 per square foot
- Engineered wood—$4 to $9 per square foot
- Laminate—$3 to $7 per square foot
- Vinyl—$2 to $7 per square foot
- Luxury vinyl—$5 to $10 per square foot
- Stone—$3 to $10 per square foot
- Concrete—$4 to $8 per square foot
- Ceramic tiles—$1 to $5 per square foot
- Porcelain tiles—$3 to $10 per square foot
- Linoleum—$3 to $10 per square foot

Climate should also be a factor in your decision-making. Hardwood floors can expand and contract with humidity. You should always let the floorboards sit for a couple of days before installation to allow them to settle evenly. You can use a humidistat or hydrometer to test the levels of humidity in your home. The ideal range is 35 percent to 55 percent to ensure a properly installed floor.

Right: If you live in an older home, you can honor the home's character by installing molding that speaks to the home's original style. It can be more expensive than, say, painting wood, but well worth the investment.

Laminate floors are for you if you're not ready to make a huge investment in flooring and want the look of hardwood without the cost; if you're just passing through and don't plan to stay in the home for very long; or if you have an active family that might wear down the floors a bit faster than others. Just be aware, laminate does feel like plastic. It isn't a complete dupe. Mimicking the character of wood with laminate is also very tricky. With engineered hardwood, you can continue the natural design of a piece of wood, but it's much more difficult to accomplish with laminate because of the way the image is printed on the materials.

Keep in mind that laminate isn't a long-term flooring solution, and you can't refinish it. And if you are looking to create a "green" home, laminate floors might not be for you. Harsh chemicals go into its production and can create health issues for someone with a chemical sensitivity.

Engineered Wood

Engineered wood flooring consists of a superthin veneer of real wood bonded to layers of plywood. Unlike hardwood, engineered wood is more resistant to moisture. It also comes in a variety of wood types, from maple and ash to oak and walnut.

Engineered wood flooring is kind of like when you go to a discount furniture store; you get the look of the real thing but for a lot less. If you don't plan to be in your home for years and years, go ahead and get an engineered wood floor; it will be a fine alternative to hardwood.

Laminate

Another flooring material to consider is laminate. Laminate is an engineered product; a photo is applied to the flooring material to give you the look of real hardwood floors. In technical terms, it's a substrate that consists of a dense fiberboard. The great thing about a laminate is that it's strong and can withstand most scratches and dents.

Opposite: Some people think you can't get a finished design with anything other than hardwood floors, but engineered wood can create an elegant effect.

For the most part, vinyl is very affordable. And you won't have a lot of stains, scratches, and dents because vinyl flooring is waterproof, which makes it a great choice for a basement or bathroom. But keep in mind that it's not real wood, meaning you can't refinish it and you can't stain it. What you see is what you get. You also need to take into account that if one of those tiles gets damaged, you are going to have to replace it. As a rule of thumb, buy an extra case. This way, if the need arises, you can pull a tile up and easily replace it.

One great thing about sealed stone floors is that if you live in a warmer climate, the floors stay much cooler and more resistant to fading and dust.

Remember to also select a grout color. Many people think you have just white and black to choose between, but you can get grout in a rainbow of colors, everything from bright blue to pale pink. If you want to feel a little freer in your color palette, choose a complementary color to go with your tile selection.

Vinyl

People use vinyl flooring for all types of installations because you can basically stick it over the current floor. Again, it gives you the look of hardwood at a much lower cost and is super easy to install yourself. It's also a fantastic option if you need to replace your floors but have yet to decide on a replacement or are renting.

Luxury vinyl is a step up within the vinyl category, made of multiple layers of vinyl that have been bonded together. The design still features a printed image on top, but it's also durable with several cushy layers. It's going to feel nicer underfoot than just a laminate floor, which you place right on top of concrete.

Stone

I once redesigned a restaurant in Harlem, New York, and installed a stone floor without realizing that if you don't seal the stone properly, it starts to take on a natural patina, fading and changing color. It's one of those things that some people like and some don't.

But unlike hardwood floors, which often fade over time with the sun and can get damaged if, say, salt from snow gets tracked inside, sealed stone is not fazed by the elements. On the negative side, however, natural stone often costs more. Also, if something heavy, like a cast-iron pan, drops onto it, the stone can crack or break, and then it's done for. All these factors should be taken into consideration when making your decision.

Above: Lean into the style of home that you have. For this Spanish-style home, we went with terra-cotta tiles in the entryway, which work well to keep the floor cool in warmer weather.

One of the negatives of concrete is that it can get costly. Much work and prep go into installing concrete, including how it's poured and laid out. Also, concrete is not very forgiving. Make sure there are no shoe prints or other imperfections on your beautiful new floors when they're being installed, or you will never be able to fix or unsee the marks.

As with stone, you must seal concrete flooring, especially in a kitchen where oil and other cooking substances will otherwise result in unsightly stains.

A plus for concrete is that, like with tile floors, you can add heated elements. This is a lovely and luxurious perk during those long winter months, especially if you live in a cold climate. Linoleum floors are sustainable and environmentally friendly. Make sure to apply a wax finish for protection.

Concrete

Concrete is another alternative to hardwood. You can customize it to get the desired shade. Concrete is going to give you a modern feel, so whether you live in New York City or Charlotte, North Carolina, you can still have the look and feel of a sleek, newly built home. Concrete is also durable and very easy to maintain.

Concrete floors are great heat conductors. Whatever the environment, concrete floors are going to lock it in. For example, if it's hot outside, concrete will keep things warmer inside, too. And if it's on the cooler side, your home will also be cool. This is why your climate is an essential factor to ponder when deciding on your floor material. You will need to reseal the concrete every year or so just to retain the look of your investment.

Ceramic and Porcelain Tiles

Typically, there are two types of tile floors: ceramic and porcelain. Porcelain is harder and less porous than ceramic, and costs a bit more.

Tile floors give a classic, iconic look. They are very durable and waterproof and will last for many, many years. Both types of tile are great for bathroom flooring and showers.

Something to factor into your costs: unless you are a master DIYer, you will need to call in an expert to install either type of tile.

Linoleum

We're all familiar with checkered linoleum floors, most often seen in entryways and kitchens. Linoleum flooring is typically sold in either single tiles or sheets. Single tiles look better. The sheets don't have a defined seam, giving them a less expensive look. A little backstory: made from linseed oil and other wood products, linoleum floors are then fused together with ground cork dust, pine resin, sawdust, and a canvas backing to make the flooring.

Grandma was on to something—there's a reason her linoleum held up so well over the years and still looks brand-new. If you place the flooring in an area of the home that doesn't get as much use, it can last a very long time. And it has an old-school charm and feel.

Grounding a room refers to giving your eyes a place to rest amid the decor. It helps to mute the noise of a room and make it less busy.

We're Looking for the Perfect Rug, Baby!

To me, rugs are practical. They're designed to make the environment cozy. But they do more than that. They also provide color, texture, and tone to a space. The main factors to consider when selecting a rug are the placement, size, and material.

If you are renting, area rugs are ideal for adding depth to a room, masking otherwise unsightly floors, and grounding a room. If the room has wall-to-wall carpet, unless you are removing the carpet, I suggest forgoing rugs. I'm not one to layer rugs over carpets.

On the following pages, you'll find my rug guidelines by room.

Opposite: Selecting the right rug for your space doesn't have to be overwhelming. Look for one that blends with the color, design, and texture of your room without getting too matchy-matchy.

If you want to go quiet with your color scheme, go high texture with your rug. It'll make your space feel more layered and lived-in.

SMOKE AND MIRRORS

Scale is so important in rug selection. The larger the rug, the better, but you also don't want the room to look like a huge dance floor with all the furniture sitting in the middle. You want to arrange the furnishings in a manner that complements the scale of the rug.

In larger rooms, it's a good idea to fit all
the furniture on the rug when you can
to help ground the space.

Living Room

The living room is typically the first room you see when you enter your home, making the rug selection for that space in your forever home important. It's not that you can't replace a rug in the span of your time living in your home, and you can certainly take it with you if you move, but rugs can be expensive, and selecting a quality one cuts down on costs in the long run.

Ideally, the front legs of your sofa and any chairs should be on the rug. If you are in a small space, just the front two legs can land on the rug, but I prefer all four legs on the rug. If it's a large space, I ensure the rug accommodates all the furniture.

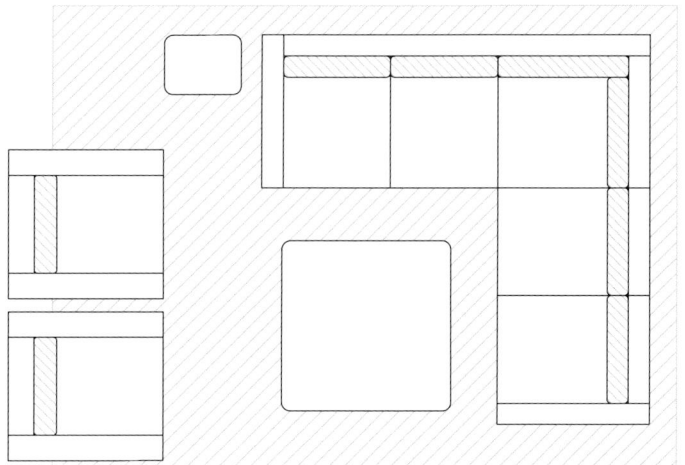

9' x 12' rug

Opposite: When you can't get all the furniture on the rug, you can cheat it by fitting the front legs.

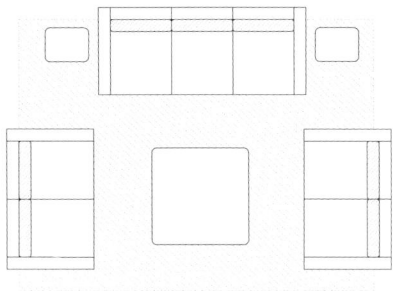

9' x 12' rug

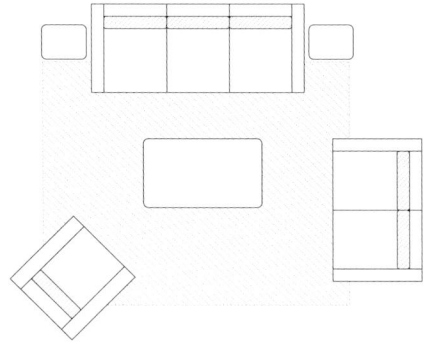

8' x 10' rug

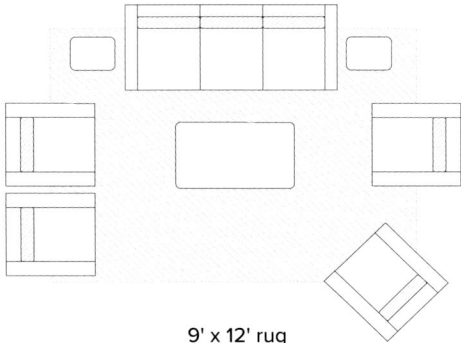

9' x 12' rug

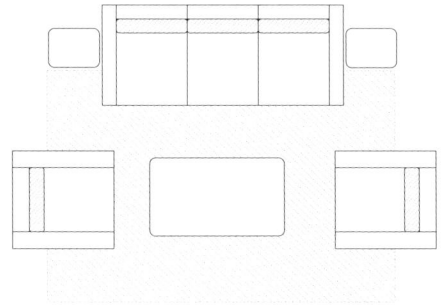

8' x 10' rug

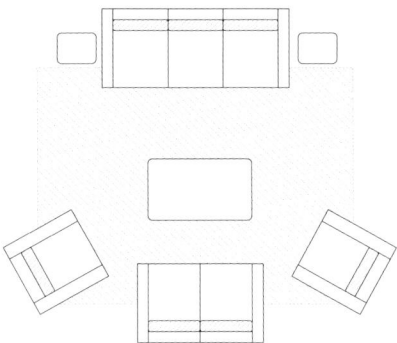

9' x 12' rug

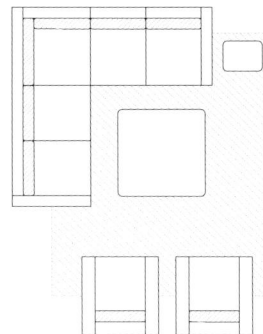

8' x 10' rug

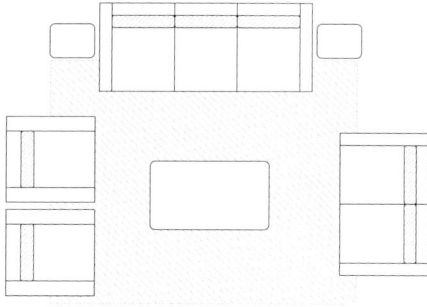

8' x 10' rug

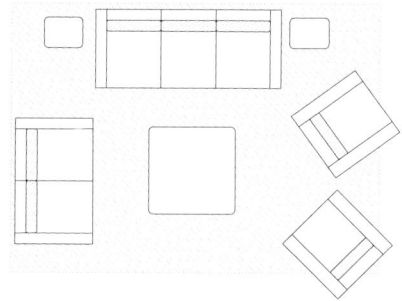

10' x 14' rug

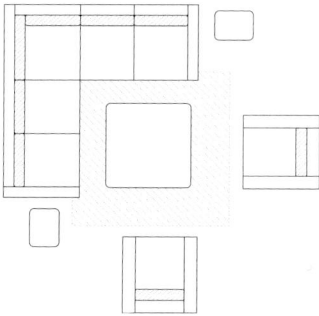

10' x 10' rug

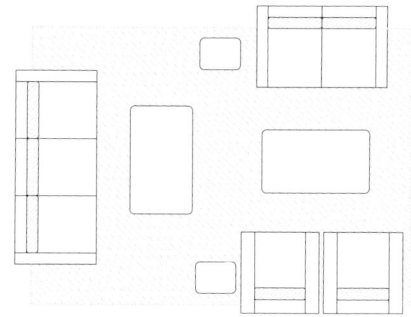

10' x 14' rug

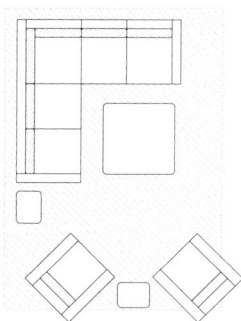

10' x 14' rug

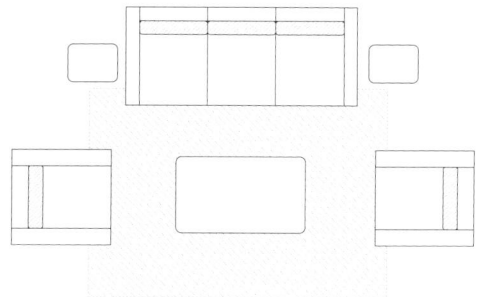

6' x 9' rug

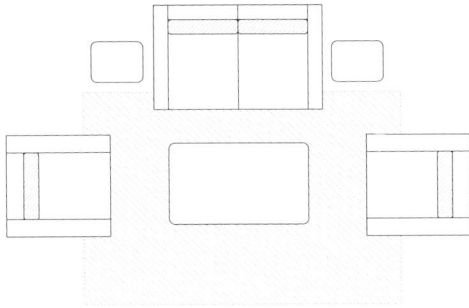

6' x 9' rug

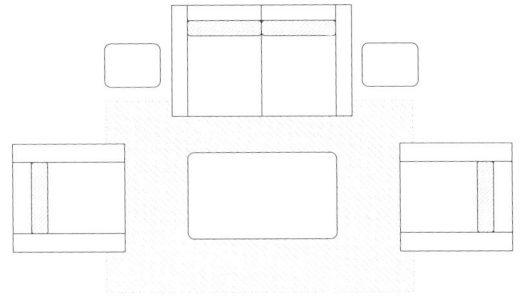

5' x 8' rug

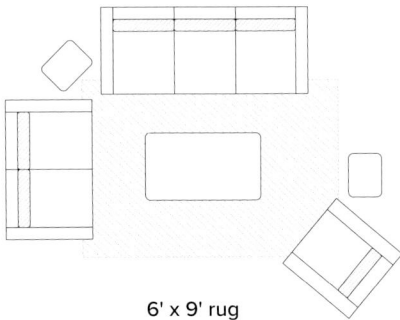

6' x 9' rug

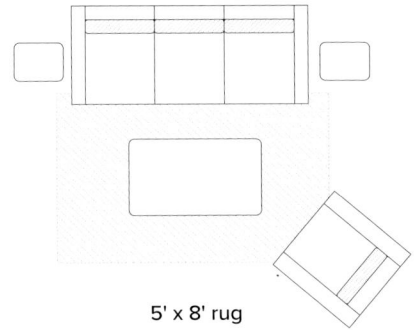

5' x 8' rug

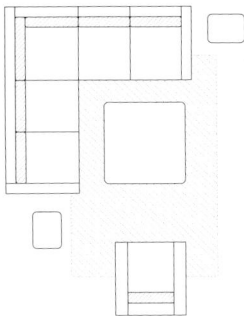

6' x 9' rug

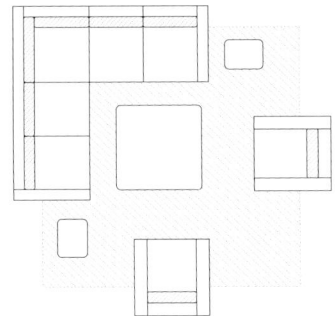

6' x 6' rug

Before you go shopping for a rug, measure your dining table and room if you haven't already for your design bible.

Dining Room

If you ever want to disrupt the internet, talk about rugs in the dining room. It's very much a personal preference, but I don't think every dining room should have a rug. I get it—food falls; wine or juice spills. You don't always want a rug there, especially if you have young kids. But if you do prefer to have a rug, you want to make sure it can comfortably fit the table and chairs.

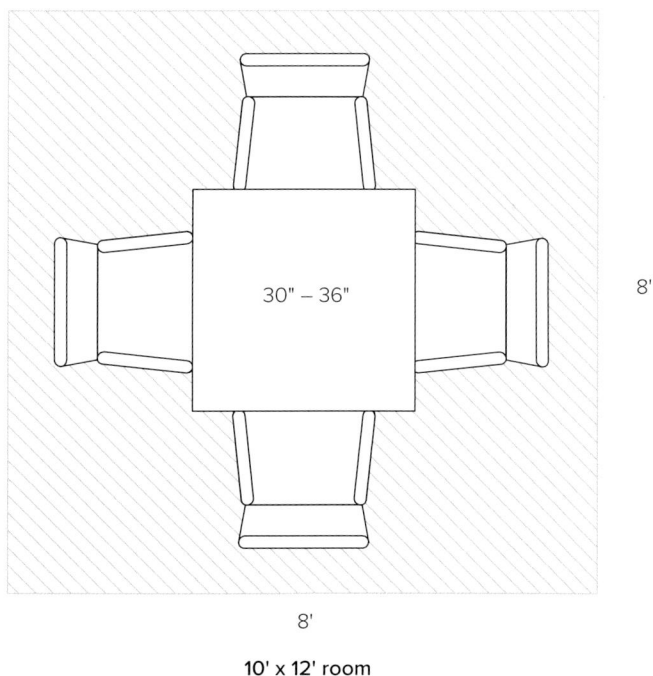

30" – 36"

8'

8'

10' x 12' room

Opposite: When choosing a rug for the dining table, go for a smooth pile so the chairs will easily pull out and push in.

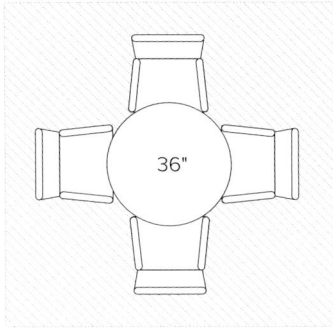

36"

8'

8'

10' x 12' room

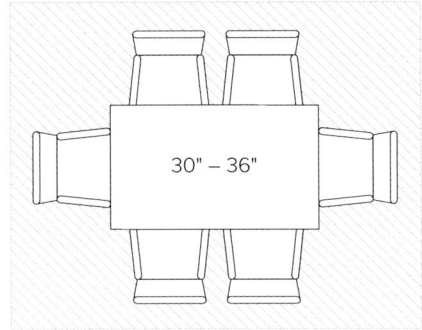

30" – 36"

8'

10'

12' x 16' room

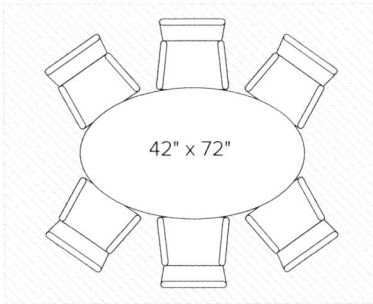

42" x 72"

8'

10'

12' x 16' room

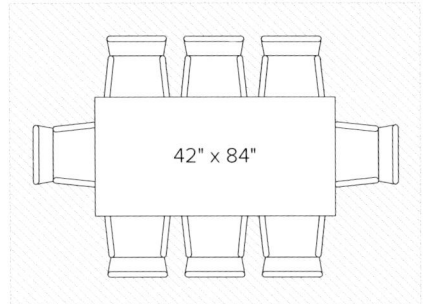

42" x 84"

9'

12'

12' x 16' room

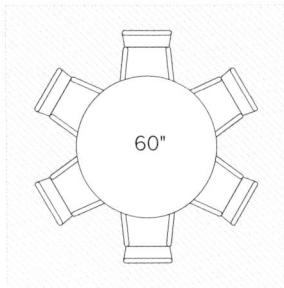

60"

10'

10'

12' x 16' room

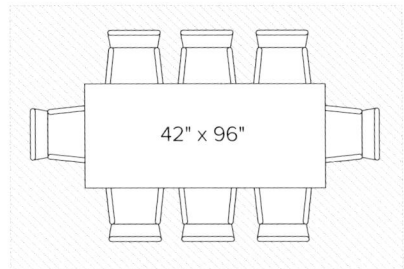

42" x 96"

9'

12' – 13'

14' x 16' room

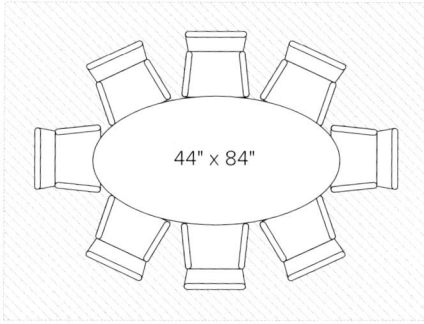

44" x 84"

9'

12'

14' x 16' room

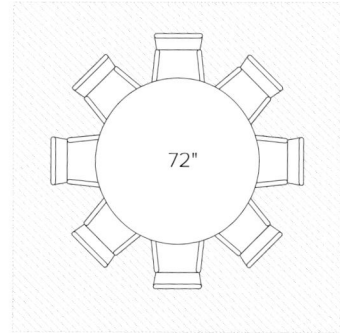

72"

12'

12'

14' x 16' room

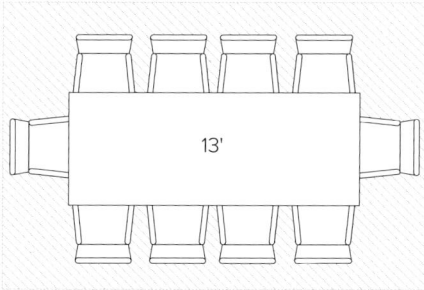

13'

9'

42" x 108"

14' x 16' room

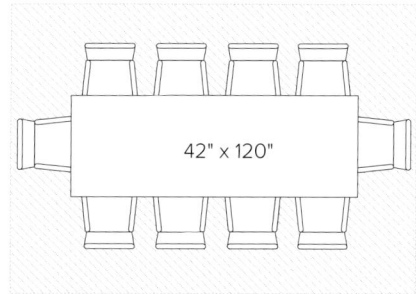

42" x 120"

10'

14'

14' x 16' room

Make sure your rug is large enough to go under the bed, with a nightstand on either side of the bed on the rug as well.

In a small room, the rug should cover about a third of the floor, and your nightstands can be placed off the rug on the floor. You want a third of the rug under the bed, from the foot of the bed to the middle of the mattress.

Bedroom

You want a nice texture or something soft for your feet to land on when you get out of bed. So just keep texture and size in mind when you're shopping for a rug for your bedroom.

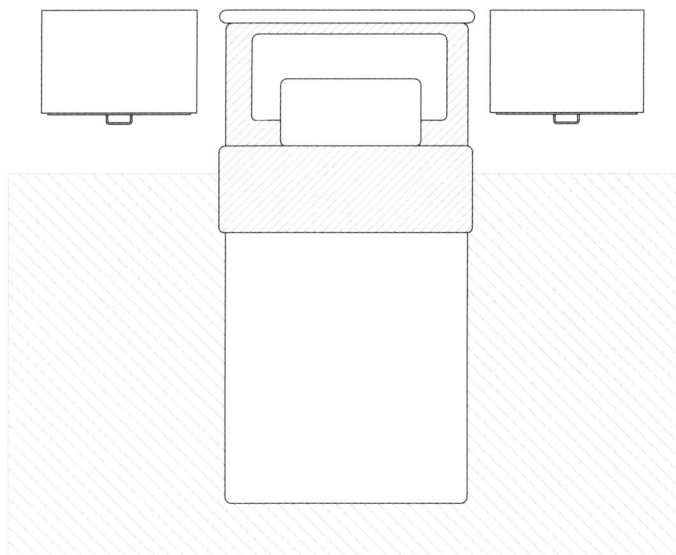

5' x 8' rug

Twin

Opposite: When a room is small, a large rug can fill it and make the space feel bigger yet cozy.

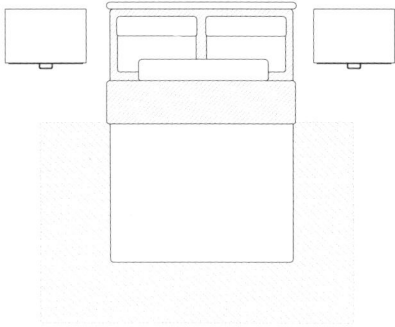

5' x 8' rug

Full / Queen

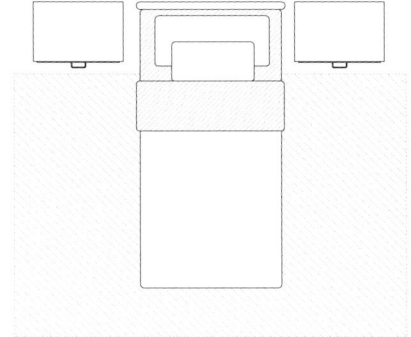

6' x 9' rug

Twin

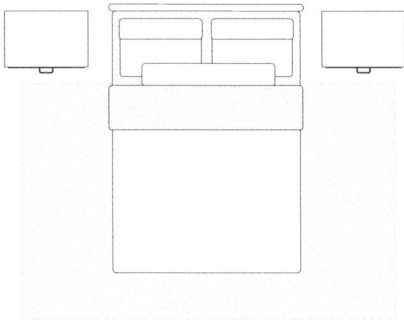

6' x 9' rug

Full / Queen

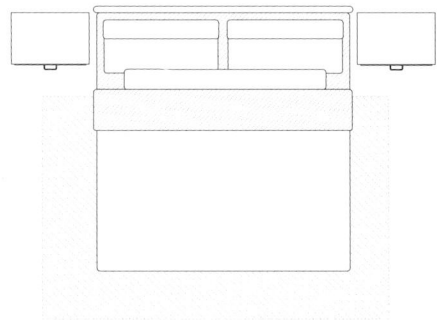

6' x 9' rug

King

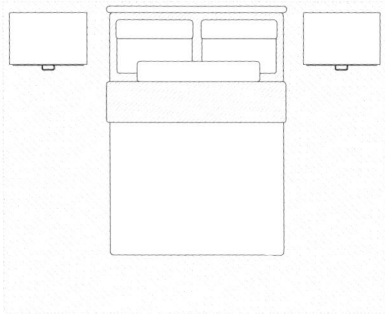

8' x 10' rug

Full / Queen

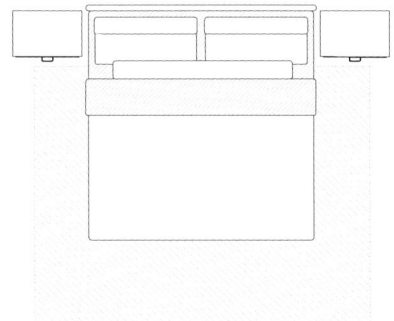

8' x 10' rug

King

WHAT RUG MATERIAL SHOULD I SELECT?

Natural Fibers
- Jute—great indoors and out; weather resistant; long-lasting; needs to be cleaned often; is a bit rough underfoot
- Silk sisal—very common in high-traffic areas
- Wool—will hide imperfections and any soiled areas; won't have to be cleaned as often

Synthetic Fibers
- Acrylic
- Polyester
- Polyurethane
- Synthetic silks
- Artificial silks—viscose, bamboo, and silk

All of these options are easy to clean, stain resistant, and affordable.

Kitchen and Entryway

The layout of both kitchens and entryways tends to fall into the same category: long and narrow. Typically, we see runners in these spaces, along with an island or a console table.

When picking a runner, my general rule of thumb is that it should be at least 70 percent of the length of the space. So if I have 100 inches to work with, I want the runner to be at least 70 inches.

SMOKE AND MIRRORS

One thing we love to do on set is layer rugs. You will constantly see jute rugs layered with a traditional rug or with an animal hide on top, often sitting at different angles. Simply moving the rug layers around can give your forever home a simple refresh. It adds a little more texture to your space. Since the cost of rugs goes up as you get a larger size, opt for a small rug as your grounding center rug and then apply the layered look with other smaller rugs, giving you the illusion of a larger rug and saving you money in the end.

Opposite: For a more modern and contemporary kitchen, keep the rug selection neutral. It will balance the space and blend into the design.

If you just want to know how your rugs will fill the space, use painter's tape and map it out on the floor to get a good visual of how it will look.

Don't forget to buy rug pads! Especially in high-traffic areas, they will help prevent you (and little ones) from slipping. If you're buying a rug online, you are usually given the option to purchase the correct size pad simultaneously at checkout.

When selecting a rug, take note of the pile. The shorter the pile, the better for a high-traffic area. Think about shag rugs: these have a very long pile and are not suitable for a high-traffic area. The longer the pile, the more insulated it will also be, offering more warmth and sound absorption.

With synthetic rugs, you can spot clean, steam clean, or vacuum, and they should clean up easily and without much trouble. With a wool rug, however, you will need to blot a stain to remove it. Be sure to use a towel that is a similar color to the rug and don't rub, so the towel and rug colors don't transfer to each other, making the stain worse.

With cotton and silk rugs, you will need to hire a professional cleaner. It's going to be an added expense that can accumulate quickly. Keep that in mind when making your selections and deciding what your needs are. Sometimes it's cheaper to get a new rug than to have a rug professionally cleaned. Consider your lifestyle and what's best for you and your family.

Above, right, and opposite: A flat woven rug, typically made of natural fibers like cotton or wool, is both informal and inviting. A stripe in the rug could introduce a new color or pattern element in a room that leans neutral.

Doubling up on hardware is great for those large, heavy drawers that house items like pots and pans. This is when you might use two knobs or two smaller pulls on one drawer.

Hardware

Selecting hardware for the kitchen cabinetry, bathroom, and entryway is hard for everyone. Even I occasionally get stumped because there are hundreds of choices on the market. If you are building new cabinets, you'll need to decide early on if you prefer knobs, pulls, or a combination of both. There are two main points to consider when making your decision. The first is functionality and what makes sense for your cabinet doors, and the second is simply preference. If you have your heart set on a certain set of pulls or knobs that doesn't work with your cabinets, there might be a piece of furniture where you could use the hardware. Don't feel like it's a lost cause at this point.

If you are replacing existing hardware, you have fewer decisions to make, which is great if you are a renter. Save the knobs you are replacing and take yours with you to your next place.

Opposite and on page 163: In this kitchen, square knobs were selected for the cabinets to mirror all the angles in the room.

KNOBS VS. PULLS

- Knobs have a smaller profile and are the most cost-efficient. You can also use knobs on drawers and cabinets. Knobs are easier to replace than pulls.
- Pulls are larger and make a bolder statement. They are the more expensive option. If you are replacing pulls, you'll need a plan because of the holes left in the cabinet or drawer. You'll need to make sure your measurements are done properly so that everything lines up.

Don't get too attached to a pull without knowing the exact measurements you will need. You could end up with extra holes in your cabinetry, and depending on the type of cabinets you have, it might be difficult to fill the holes. Also, make sure the screws supplied with the pulls or knobs are long enough for the thickness of the cabinet or drawer that will house them. This is an easy fix, but still, you'll save yourself time and energy if you already know the length that you will need to secure the hardware.

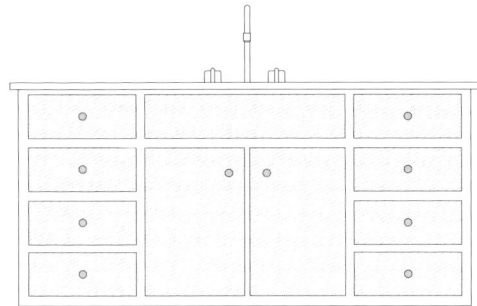

All knobs

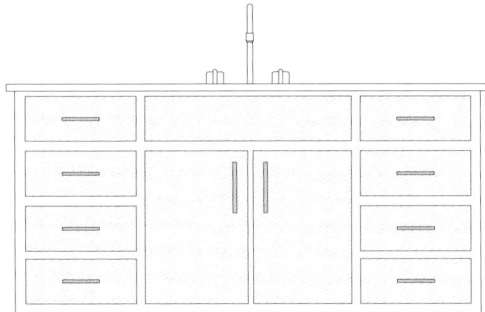

All pulls

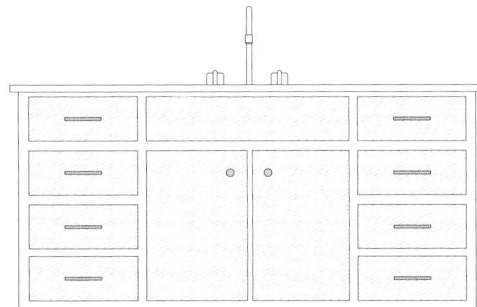

Knobs + pulls

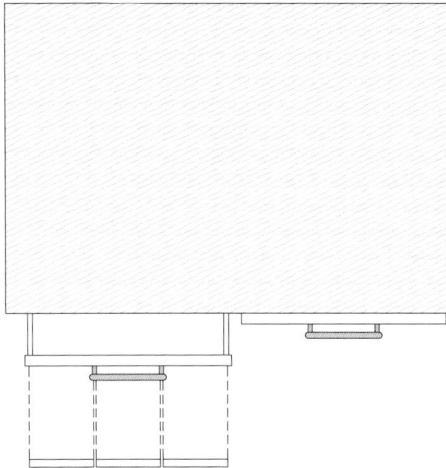

In general, a 1:3 pull-to-drawer
ratio works best

 3" to 4" pull

 1" knob

Small drawers 12" or less

 8" or more pull

 Two pulls

 Two knobs

Large drawers 10" to 48"

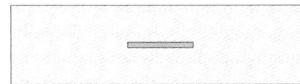 4" to 8" pull

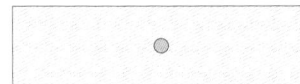 1" to 1.5" knob

Medium drawers 12" to 30"

Opposite: When selecting fixtures and
hardware, don't be afraid to mix metals.
Here, we went with brass accents on
the pendants and barstools, and classic
silver for the cabinet hardware.

- Ceramic
- Chrome
- Copper
- Glass
- Wood

Complement Your Space with Hardware

When selecting styles of hardware, think about what will complement your space. For instance, if you have a more traditional design, then you want to stick with ridges, curved silhouettes, and a textured detail, something more classic. If you prefer modern cabinetry and your home is contemporary, you want to go with clean lines, minimal design, and a sleek profile.

GENERAL GUIDELINES WHEN CHOOSING SIZES FOR YOUR HARDWARE

- Pull length should be approximately one-third of the cabinet or drawer width. For a small drawer, 12 inches or less, I recommend using a long pull, 3 to 4 inches wide, or a knob with a 1-inch diameter.

- If you have medium drawers, which range from 12 to 30 inches, select a long pull between 4 and 8 inches. If you prefer a knob, select one between 1 inch and 1½ inches in diameter.

- For large drawers, between 30 and 48 inches, opt for a longer pull, at least 8 inches long. For a knob, select one at least 1 inch in diameter; 1½ inches is ideal.

The Role of Materials

In terms of materials and finish, consider how the hardware will contrast in the room. If your home style tends to align with warmer tones, brass will work best. It will give you a more vintage feel.

Cooler tones work best with darker hardware, like matte black or oil-rubbed bronze. Try to match the hardware throughout your forever home for a sleek, clean look. But don't feel like you must follow the rules. Mix up your hardware selections and styles for what suits you and your home.

Opposite: Center your hardware on the face of the drawers. This will balance the room and give your eyes a place to rest.

- Upper cabinets: Knobs or pulls should be 2½ to 3 inches from the bottom edge of your cabinet door.
- Lower cabinets: Knobs or pulls should be 2½ to 3 inches from the top edge of your cabinet door.
- Drawers: Knob or pulls should be centered horizontally on the face of the drawer.

Ensure that you have consistent placement of either knobs or pulls throughout the room. If you are working with new cabinetry, you can do a mock-up of the cabinets with blue painter's tape to ensure that you have the exact measurements correct before drilling.

If you haven't yet selected your hardware, you can mark the screw holes on the tape and take that with you to the hardware store for the exact size you will need for those specific doors or drawers. Make sure you aren't marking the width of the cabinet pull but instead measuring the screw holes.

The Workhorse of the Home

Why do we all end up in the kitchen at a party? I'll tell you why—the kitchen is the backbone of a home. You might have a formal living room that no one has used in weeks, but a kitchen is used multiple times a day by everyone who lives in the home (and their guests).

People open and close cabinets many times a day. For this reason, you want to spend the extra money for high-quality materials for your cabinets. You need durability. The same goes for the knobs and pulls. If you want metal, select a solid metal knob or pull. You don't want to deal with chips or wear over time. Pay a little extra to get quality pieces rather than having to replace a less expensive version down the road.

SMOKE AND MIRRORS

If you are dealing with older cabinets that have previously drilled holes, you can cover those holes by selecting pulls or knobs with backplates. You will still have a streamlined look to your cabinetry but with a cover that houses the imperfections. Backplates will also add a little dimension to the hardware. Backplates can be found in a variety of metals, so surely, you'll find one to match your knobs or pulls.

Opposite: These knob selections mirror the trim of the cabinet. It's a subtle detail but one that helps to achieve a cohesive look.

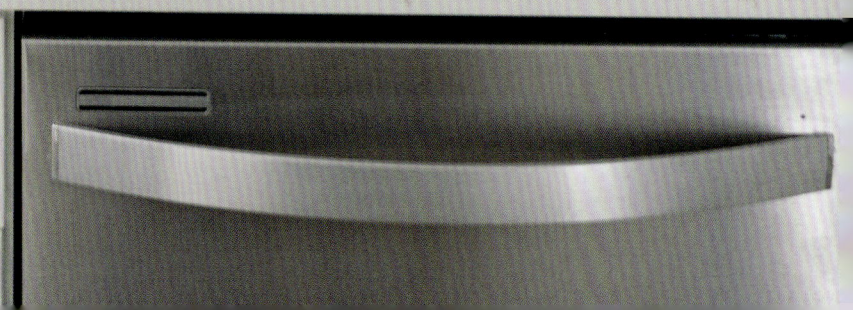

SMOKE AND MIRRORS

Peel-and-stick wallpaper and tiles are a fantastic way to camouflage problem areas when you have exhausted all your funds on purchasing a home. You may not want to hire a contractor, and this is a great tool for making some improvements yourself. You can get peel-and-stick subway tiles to cover up an unsightly kitchen backsplash; they're wipeable and highly durable. Fun extra tip: you can even use peel-and-stick covers for old, worn-down appliances like refrigerators and stoves. They come in a wide range of styles.

I Say Drapery When I'm Feeling Fancy

Let's clear something up—curtains and drapery are the same thing. I say drapery when I feel fancy and drapes when keeping it informal, but I don't want to confuse you. Both words are interchangeable with *curtains*.

There are so many different styles of drapes—high-end, elegant, extremely casual, and somewhere in the middle. They can be custom-made, or you can buy off-the-rack panels. You can get blackout curtains, which are perfect in a bedroom and allow in no light. The material is also just as varied. Your selection will be what works best for you and your home, but if you measure the windows and know what light conditions you want to control, you can narrow down your options reasonably quickly by selecting the material first.

The most common questions I get about window treatments are "What length should I select?" and "What material should I choose?" There are thousands of options, and I get it; making these decisions can feel overwhelming. Let's break down the choices.

Window treatments are essentially grouped into three different categories:

- **Hard window treatments made from wood or vinyl:** shades, blinds, and shutters

- **Soft window treatments:** drapery, sheers, swags, valances, and roman shades

- **Layered window treatments:** a mix of both hard and soft window treatments

Opposite: Oftentimes people don't know what kind of window treatments to use for French doors or sliding glass doors, but you can never go wrong with ceiling-to-floor drapes. Go for a sheer material or lightweight linen to let the sun stream through.

If you are using ring clips, your curtains will come down at least an extra inch and a half. Keep this in mind when you are measuring.

After installing your curtain rod, attach painter's tape or craft paper to the rod itself and let the tape or paper run to the floor. This allows you to measure properly and get a rough visual of what the curtains will feel like in your space. You can go from there to make your selection.

Drapery 101

Most designers, me included, want to take the drapery rod up as high as we can. This allows your space to feel taller and more dramatic. Measure 2 to 6 inches from the ceiling and install the rod in the wall. As for on the sides, go 6 to 12 inches past the window casing.

The drapery should go all the way to the floor, so measure accordingly. The fabric can kiss the floor or form a 1-inch puddle, but at the very least, it should be touching the floor.

With any drapery style, you will need to basically double the width of your window with your fabric. For instance, if your window is 100 inches wide, you will need your drapery to be 180 to 200 inches wide. You can either find a large panel or double up with two panels on either side of the window, creating a fuller look.

SMOKE AND MIRRORS

Steve Harvey loves details, and he loves expensive, lush drapery. When I worked for him, I didn't always have the budget to supply custom drapes, so I would buy two shorter panels of the same drape and take them to a dry cleaner or tailor to have them sewn together and turned into one long panel. You will want to buy four panels, and for about $20 in alternations, you can have long, dramatic drapes.

When buying panels off the rack, get panels that are longer than what you need. Then have your local dry cleaner hem them to the right size for a custom feel at a more affordable price.

Opposite: The very best look is when drapery just kisses the floor.

PANELS AND PLEATS, OH MY!

Single-Panel Drapery
Single-panel curtains are designed to cover the entire window but need a little help to avoid looking like a sheet. A tieback is a nice option for the single panel, creating a more classic, open look. This choice works well with a small window or in a narrow area of your home. When used on a smaller window, the panel fills the space nicely.

Pinch-Pleat Drapery
Pinch pleats are a timeless drapery detail, with the fabric pinched at the top, near the rod, creating the look of pleats. This treatment is usually reserved for heavier fabrics, such as wool or velvet.

Box-Pleat Drapery
The box pleat is when the fold runs deep and is uninterrupted. You get full coverage from this style. It is usually found in a dining room or a bedroom.

Goblet Pleats
Goblet pleats get their name because when you take a step back, they resemble a wineglass. Very dramatic and over-the-top, they are most often seen in a very formal setting and rooms with high ceilings.

Pencil Pleats
For a more casual, thinner pleat, you can select the pencil pleat. It feels less stuffy and more approachable.

Tab Panels
When done right, tab panels have a sweet, nostalgic throwback aesthetic. Perfect for a kitchen or a bathroom, or in a farmhouse- or cottage-style home.

Opposite: Typically, I take the drapes all the way to the ceiling, but in a room with a vaulted ceiling, I opt to go slightly higher than the window casing, at least a foot above the window.

Inverted Pleat

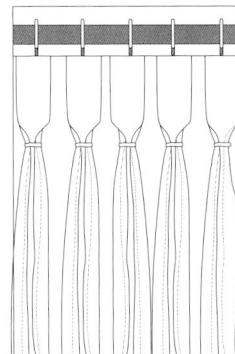

Goblet Pleat

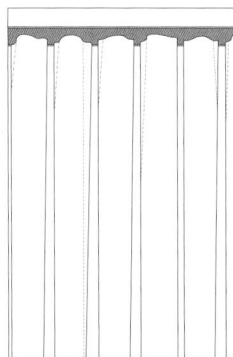

Ripple Fold

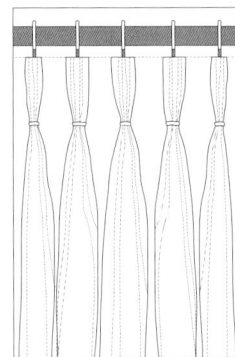

Pinch Pleat

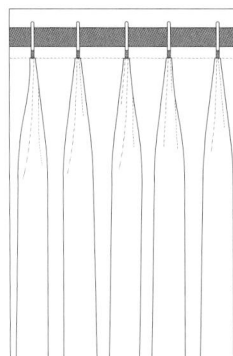

Tailored Pleat

Cubicle

QUESTIONS TO ASK
YOURSELF WHEN DECIDING
ON A CURTAIN ROD

- What room will it be used in?
- What is the window size?
- How frequently will I be opening and closing the curtains?
- How does the metal finish work with the rest of the room?
- What finials or end caps would I like on the rod?
- Is a tension rod the best option for a smaller window?
- Will double curtain rods work, to layer two different types of drapery?
- Are panel tracks for me?
- Would motorized curtains work in my home?

Drapery on Panel Track

Reserved for big picture windows and sliding doors, a panel track makes for easy maneuverability of your window treatment. For a very sleek, clean look, you can recess panel tracks into the ceiling, if you so choose. It's very tailored and allows for beautiful drapery to complete the look.

Sheer Curtains

Sheer curtains offer a translucent feel, allowing light to pass through while still offering a little privacy. Sheer curtains pair very well with heavier drapery for a complete look.

Café Curtains

Often found in a bathroom or a kitchen, café curtains traditionally fill the lower half of a window. Sunlight can still make its way through the window, but the space feels more private.

SMOKE AND MIRRORS

For a budget café curtain alternative, turn fun vintage napkins or dish towels into café curtains. Use curtain loops with clips on an inexpensive tension rod for an easy, chic look.

Opposite: Bay windows can be tricky for hanging curtains, so opt for a panel track to give a continuous look.

- Measure window sizes and heights.
- Consider drapery rod placement and ensure proper clearance from ceiling and walls.
- Double-check all drapery measurements before installation.
- Consider different drapery hardware styles, such as curtain rods, tension rods, and double curtain rods.

Shutters

Typically, wood window shutters are either louvered or have fixed slats and are attached with hinges for easy opening and closing. Shutters provide light control and privacy. They're beautiful and have a lot of vintage charm. A comparable soft window treatment would be woven bamboo shades, which add a little dimension and texture.

Cellular Shades

A lot of people opt for cellular shades in modern homes, especially those in warm climates. These shades are not only energy efficient but also provide insulation. You can have single, double, or triple pleats, allowing you the ability to dictate just how much light filters into the space.

Roman Shades

Roman shades hang flat when lowered, and when raised, they pull into a pleated look. You have both privacy and light control with these shades. Roller shades would fall into the same category as roman shades. Easy, but also economical. A valance can cover the Roman or roller shade housing at the top of your window.

SMOKE AND MIRRORS

You want to invest in good-quality shades that will see a lot of use—such as in the bedroom where you need to close the shades for privacy at night but open them for light during the day. That's when buying cheap can be expensive. But feel free to save on shades that you likely won't touch that often, like in the kitchen and dining room, where you're more likely to keep them open all the time.

Opposite: The flat panel roman shade is the most classic style, one you'll never get tired of.

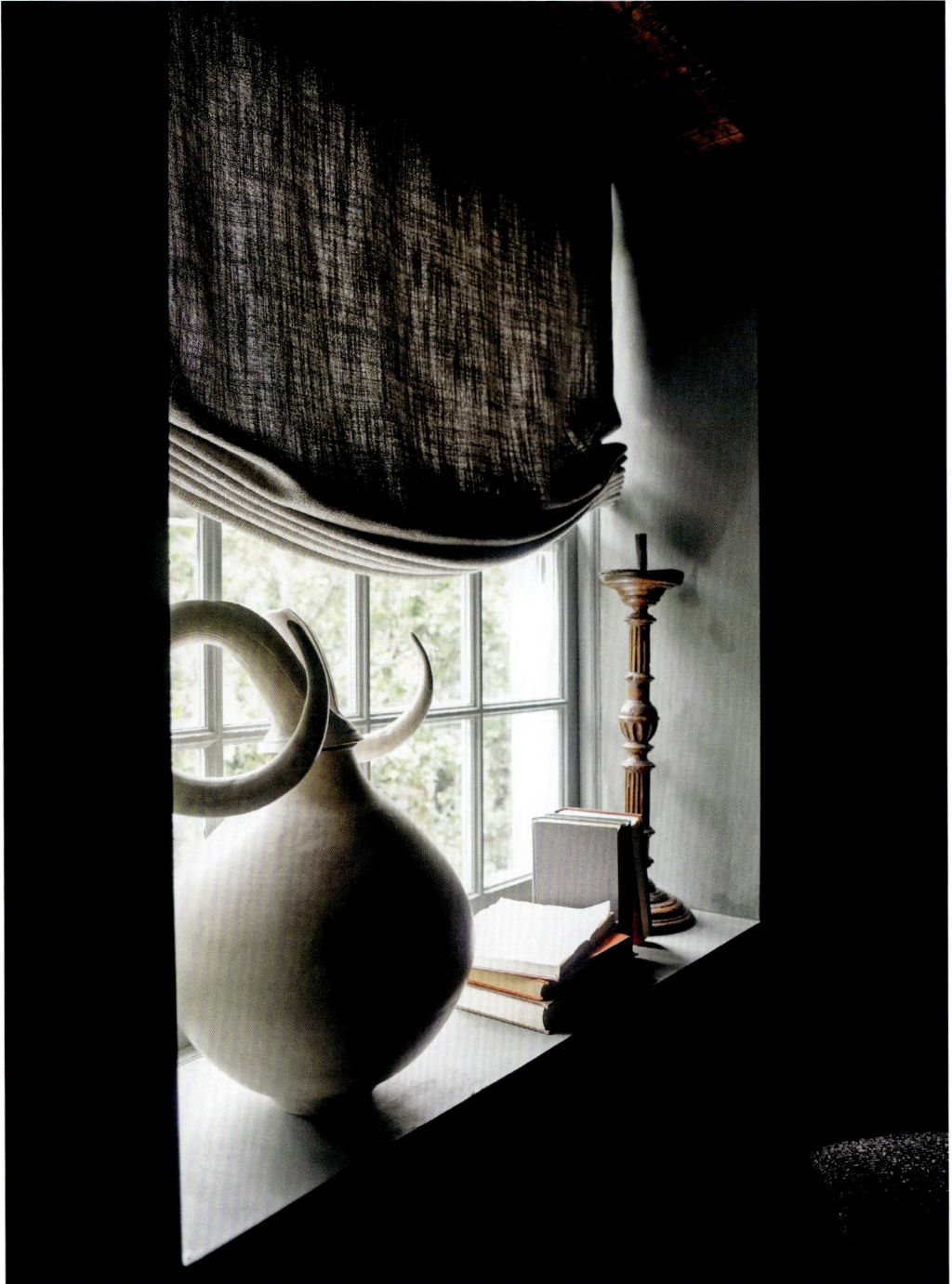

Above: The relaxed roman shade is my personal favorite with its effortless elegance.

Plain Fold

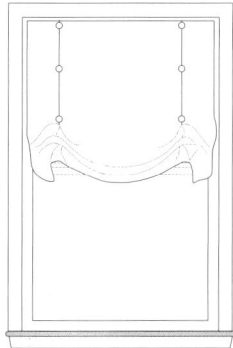

Swag

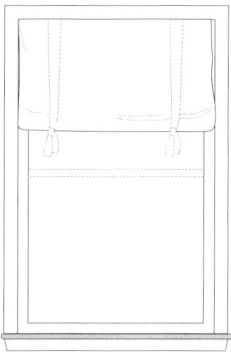

Tie

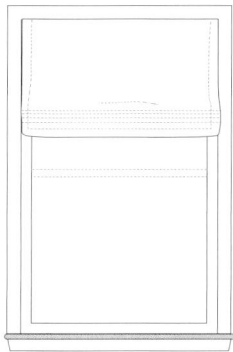

Flat Fold

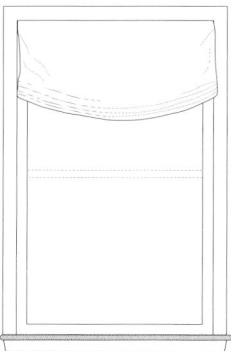

Relaxed (European)

Soft Fold

WHEN IN ROMAN

Roman shades come in a few different styles. Choose what's right for your room based on style and function.

Plain Fold

This is your standard roman shade style. It's iconic and classic—great in bedrooms as a blackout shade, which is ideal for keeping out the light.

Swag

Go granny-chic with this more decorative shade that's perfect for kitchens or reading nooks or other windows that you're not planning to open and close very often.

Tie

A tie style looks right at home in the kitchen above a sink or in a powder room. Like the swag, go for this when you want a more decorative style.

Flat Fold

A more minimalist style than the plain fold, this shade has no horizontal creases visible when the shade is open or raised halfway. It could easily go in a living room or a bedroom, where you want a little more privacy.

Relaxed (European)

The holy grail of them all, the relaxed has a casual sophistication. It's better with lighter weight fabrics like linen, which helps you get a good swag. It works well for small windows; anything too big will look like a theater curtain.

Soft Fold

This more formal style will showcase its fluffy layers when pulled up. A style your mother or grandmother will totally approve of, it should be saved for the dining room or a formal living room (if that's your thing).

When considering materials, think about how the furniture or textile will be used. High-traffic areas require more durable fabric. On the other hand, you can go with more delicate fabric for the lesser-used items in low-traffic areas.

High-Traffic Items
- Sofa used daily
- Kitchen barstools
- Bedding
- Cushioned chair

Low-Traffic Items
- Formal dining room chairs
- Accent pillows
- Ottomans
- Curtains

Let's Talk About Fabrics

And honey, you thought we were done . . . I know you are thinking, *Mikel, how are we still talking about the varied decisions we need to make?* Trust me, we aren't done, and yes, you still have more decisions to make.

When I'm selecting fabrics for interior design projects, I look at factors such as atmosphere, living situation, functionality, and durability. I want you to give thought to the same details I do. High-traffic areas will need a different fabric than a low-traffic room. Think about the atmosphere and the tones throughout the room; think about the context of the space and how you will layer items. You want to make sure the fabrics work with one another, that they are telling your story. Texture, color, and pattern are your best friends when you are choosing any type of fabric to put into a house.

If you are a family with children and pets and you are dealing with a lot of stains, you might want to consider an outdoor fabric, such as those by Sunbrella, that also lends itself well to indoor furniture—fabric that can be easily wiped clean. Selecting a fabric with lots of texture where spills blend in is another option.

Think about the very vivid and busy pattern on the carpet of a hotel or airport. It's pretty, but it's also meant to conceal stains and spills.

You can also do what I call the "rub test" to check fabric durability. It's simply taking two pieces of fabric and rubbing them together; you want to see if either fabric sheds or pills. What is their compatibility with one another? Knowing this will tell you how they will live together in your home.

SMOKE AND MIRRORS

Don't be afraid to have a few slipcovers in different colors to change your sofa's appearance seasonally. It's a simple trick that can give your space a fresh look without costing much money.

- Durability
- Functionality
- Aesthetics
- Atmosphere
- Tone
- Texture
- Color
- Pattern
- Intended use
- Cleanability

Making an Eco-Friendly Decision

We often shun poly blends and synthetic materials, but there are some beautiful synthetic fabrics that can give you the look of wool or leather. Consider materials that work best for your household when selecting fabrics and textiles.

Tried-and-True Fabric and Pattern Selections

The materials on this list are merely a suggestion of fabric choices that work in many different situations. You might not want a merino wool pillowcase the same way you might not want a linen sofa. Do what works best for you.

- Canvas
- Cashmere
- Cotton
- Damask
- Gingham
- Leather
- Linen
- Merino wool
- Polyester or a poly blend
- Silk or raw silk
- Suede
- Twill
- Velvet

Opposite: Select your sofa and armchair fabric based on your family's needs and habits. Think about the type of material, color, and durability.

Slipcovers are wonderful, and you can wash them yourselves. Just don't put them in the dryer! Taking the risk that the fabric will shrink is not worth the extra time you will need to let them air-dry.

The overall care a fabric requires should be considered before you invest in a piece for your forever home. Think about the intended use of the fabric you're selecting.

Always consider where a piece of upholstered furniture will sit in your home when choosing the fabric. Velvet is stunning, but it also fades in the sun, so think about what will be affected by natural light and what will remain in the cozy, dark spaces in your home when making your selections.

Right: Slipcovers have gotten a glow-up over the last decade. Not every cover is tied at the ends or loose-fitting like a sheet thrown over a sofa. You can find ones these days that look like high-end upholstery but are perfect for high-traffic areas.

PICK THE RIGHT FURNISHINGS

One of the best shopping lessons I learned from Emily Henderson was "If it isn't a hell yes, then it's a no." I want you to bring that energy to the design of your forever home. I want you to pick only things you love. Your taste will change over time. Honey, you might not still like that vase you bought in 2002. As a matter of fact, I hope you don't, because barring very iconic pieces, design is constantly evolving. You won't move from home to home with everything you've ever owned, but you are collecting along the way. I want you to look at items with your forever home in mind and choose items that will add value to your surroundings.

The Ins and Outs of Furnishing Your Home

When we move, we usually bring most of our furniture with us. It would be exhausting and expensive to start fresh every time, so I want you to begin cataloging your most beloved pieces and what will undoubtedly come with you to each new home.

Whether you have found a new home or started renovating one you've been in for years, turn to your design bible to reference the measurements of your sofa or headboards. See if you need to trade your barstools for chairs or if the ottoman will fit in the room. Once you have begun your editing and revisited your measurements, you are ready to get to the most fun part—shopping and styling!

SMOKE AND MIRRORS

I turn to Etsy for a lot of things, but one item on the site that I really love is wall panels. These panels can be affixed directly to the wall behind a bed, creating a beautiful, inexpensive headboard. For a theatrical look, you can use Command strips to connect multiple panels for a headboard long enough to sit behind not only the bed but also the night tables.

Opposite: Sometimes it's fun to think outside the box when it comes to furniture. Because this homeowner had plenty of storage elsewhere in the room, we brought in a marble cube to serve as the nightstand, which lends lots of character.

- Declutter any existing items you no longer wish to include in the room
- Take the time to curate furniture and decor over multiple shopping trips rather than rushing to make purchases
- Consider problem areas that could use inexpensive fixes before major renovations

The Art of the Edit

To quote Coco Chanel, "Before you leave the house, you should look in the mirror and remove one item." The same applies to design. We can't always tell intuitively if we've got one too many things going on in a space. If you must ask yourself, "Is it too much?," then it typically is. Designing a home requires identifying each room's focal point and working within existing walls and parameters. Incorporating different textures adds versatility and visual interest. Editing is vital, as is avoiding over-accessorizing.

A diverse mix of items is encouraged, and natural light sources, mirrors, and greenery should be considered to create a homey feel. Designing with personality and harmony is essential.

Ask yourself how the layout of the space will play a role in what major furniture pieces you bring into your home. In the living room, the focal point might be a large bookshelf. In the kitchen, the cabinets or an island might provide the wow factor.

Once you pin down the focal point, then you can begin to arrange your furniture and play with orientations of the furnishings in the room. We begin to see what makes sense in the space.

Opposite: The placement of the patinaed cutting boards with the vintage pitcher lends warmth and interest to the modern cabinets and marble countertop.

Declutter before you begin designing your space. See what you have and then strip the room down to the core pieces you're going to keep. This will allow you to see what you are working with.

You don't have to buy everything all at once. This is your forever home, not your must-be-finished-right-now home. A design plan takes time, and there's a lot to savor with slow design. Be intentional with where you spend your money and what you spend it on.

Opposite and above left and right:
Artfully arranged items like books, vases, and sculptures can help tell the story of who you are without adding too much clutter.

Use dimmable ceiling lights, if you can. You won't be sorry. Having the ability to control the lighting for any situation is key. Three-way lightbulbs can also be used to achieve the same ambient effect that dimmers can.

If you are moving into an older home, don't be scared to add electrical outlets to meet your needs. Or plan around the existing ones if adding more is not in the budget.

Plan your lights in a triangular formation, rather than in a straight line. If you have two side tables with lamps next to your sofa, place another lamp across from that setup, so the lamps form a triangle. You can do the same in a bedroom. If you have a sconce over each night table, place a lamp on a dresser across from your bed.

Planning Your Lighting Grid

Lighting is one of the most important elements to consider when creating your forever home. Being intentional with your lighting grid early on will set the tone quickly and easily. Consider all aspects of lighting to know what's best for you.

For the kind of low, hazy lighting you might see in your favorite restaurant or cocktail lounge, you'll want ambient lighting. Think about what you will be doing in the room; will you be writing at a desk? You will want to make sure to have a table lamp if so. Will you be reading on the sofa? Plan for a floor lamp. This is where you will be so thankful you measured everything in advance.

Consider the Natural Light

Natural light is a beautiful thing, but not all rooms have it. If you don't have a lot of light streaming into your room, consider using the art of illusion, the smoke and mirrors I'm always talking about—but this time, literally use mirrors in your space to help bounce light around. This will help to make a space appear larger. You can turn a dark hallway into a room that feels more spacious than it is.

SMOKE AND MIRRORS

Halloween is significant at *The Drew Barrymore Show*. We always try to make the set dark and moody, so I rely on dimmable lighting. Since I'm dealing with a constantly evolving set, I'm often challenged to create a set without outlets, yet I want to hang a light. An excellent hack I've learned that could be applied in your home is to modify a wall sconce so that you don't have to plug it in. Because it will have a backplate, you can cut the wiring and hang it as if you had hardwired the fixture. Then, instead of a lightbulb, use a battery-operated puck light, aka disc light. These remote-controlled, dimmable lights can be installed using Velcro or Command strips where the lightbulb typically sits. You could use this for lights down a hallway or in a tricky nook. It's simple and cost-effective.

Opposite: An oversized mirror will do wonders for bringing natural light into a darker room.

The Role of Texture

When you walk into a room and all the material of the furniture is the same or similar, it can feel flat or one-note. I like to have three different materials in a room, and that's not me being extra. For instance, in your living room, treat your sofa as the base for building texture. Think about the material of your coffee table or any chairs nearby. Think about bookshelves and other furniture items. Break things up. If you feel like you have a lot of wood pieces, consider incorporating a stone or metal coffee table and a leather chair. You want to build diversity into your furnishings. This same theory should apply when you're designing any space in your home.

In the dining room, we often see wood tables with wood chairs. Vary the textures a bit by looking for a plaster or papier-mâché vase you can put on top of the table or a rug you can layer underneath it, or put a throw over one of the chairs. That simple, subtle addition will soften the space in a way you didn't see coming.

And don't forget the greenery. This is the time to bring in plants, fresh flowers, or organic branches in a vase. Olive or eucalyptus branches can last a long time with little care, while still having a dramatic yet grounding effect. Greenery in a space is always going to make it feel alive.

Adding textures will make a space sing. Here, we chose pottery filled with eucalyptus leaves (*above*), and in the dining room (*opposite*), we added fresh flowers, fruit, and a throw.

Curate Items You Will Never Want to Let Go Of

When you fill your home with things that have real meaning to you and your family, you will instantly feel joy when you see them. I am someone who likes antiques, so I have several pieces with provenance scattered throughout the house. Each one is special to me and will move with me wherever I go. There are so many great shops to peruse, which will help you curate your forever home collection of vintage finds.

Harmonize Your Forever Home

Find unifying pieces that have the same hue when working to bring your rooms together. Staying within a set palette forces the furnishings to work together within your space. If you opt to go monochromatic, find a good balancing color to contrast within the room. For example, if you are painting the room a dusty blue, you could harmonize with sage green or rose. The colors don't have to be in the same immediate family, but make sure they're at least cousins.

SMOKE AND MIRRORS

When I was working with Steve Harvey, between taping his TV show and doing his radio show, he spent upward of thirteen hours a day in his office. It was his personal haven. That's why it was so important for him to have that space well-designed and not just look like a generic workspace. It was his home away from home. He wanted this high-end sofa from the clothing brand Fendi. As I began researching the piece, I realized that it was $30,000. I was sure he didn't want to spend $30,000. He just saw a sofa and got excited. I found a similar sofa on Wayfair, then had an upholstery shop sew some nice leather belts to the bottom to mimic the look of the Fendi piece. I was able to re-create the $30,000 sofa for around $2,000. Find inspiration and think outside the box to re-create the look yourself.

Opposite: Curate items you love, and you will create a collection that speaks to your forever home. You might not know where to display it when you find a treasure, but once you're home, you'll discover the right place for the right piece.

Hidden-Gem Shops Around the World

I love shops that push the boundaries of design and aren't afraid to present things differently, take risks—shops off the beaten path, where you find items you wouldn't expect to see paired next to each other. I love to support independent shops, thrift shops, and vintage stores alongside traditional retail stores. On page 215, I share my roundup of shops I love and support on a regular basis in projects I'm working on and in my own home.

Opposite: Checking out an impressive pendant at South Loop Loft in Chicago. Finding unique and standout pieces for my own home and for clients is one of my favorite parts of designing.

DENMARK
Studio Oliver Gustav—København

UNITED STATES

ARKANSAS
Marrs on Main—Bentonville
Pippa's Bin—Fair Oaks

CALIFORNIA
Berbere Imports—Inglewood
Forbes & Lomax—Hollywood
Gibson—Los Angeles
Olive Ateliers—Los Angeles
Rejuvenation—Los Angeles
Rose Bowl Flea Market—Pasadena
Shoppe Amber Interiors—Larkspur
Soho Home—Hollywood

FLORIDA
Arhaus—Coral Gables
Justco—Miami

GEORGIA
The Design House by HDC—Atlanta
East Fork—Atlanta
14th Street Modern & Vintage Home—
    Atlanta
Le Jardin Français—Atlanta

ILLINOIS
The Golden Triangle—Chicago
Jayson Home—Chicago
Mercantile M—Chicago
Montauk Sofa—Chicago
South Loop Loft—Chicago
Tufenkian Artisan Carpets—Chicago

MICHIGAN
Woodward Throwbacks—Detroit

NEBRASKA
Salt Creek Mercantile—Ashland

NEW YORK
The Antique Warehouse Hudson NY—
    Hudson

A.Therien—Cairo
CB2—New York City
Chelsea Flea—New York City
Cosentino—New York City
France & Son—New York City
The Gallery at 200 Lex—New York City
House of Hackney—New York City
Jamali Garden—New York City
Lawton Mull—Queens
Maison Gerard—New York City
Michael Del Piero Good Design
    Hamptons—Wainscott
Newel—New York City
Portmanteau—Queens
Preston Konrad—New York City
Quarters—New York City
RW Guild—New York City
Visual Comfort & Co.—New York City

NORTH CAROLINA
Dressing Rooms Interiors—Charlotte

TENNESSEE
The Riley/Land Collection—Smyrna
StayFoxx Studios—Chattanooga

TEXAS
Juniper & Bros.—The Woodlands

VIRGINIA
Driftwood & Moss—Onancock

LOCATIONS NATIONWIDE

Crate & Barrel
Inspired Closets
Pottery Barn
The Shade Store

LOCATIONS WORLDWIDE
Le Labo

ONLINE

Lulu and Georgia
McGee & Co.

Opposite: Here I am picking out rugs in Tufenkian Artisan Carpets (*left* and *bottom*) and vintage olive jars at Jayson Home (*top*), both in Chicago.

I love Montauk Sofa in Chicago for their
sturdy oversize sofas and custom fabric
options.

I worked with Golden Triangle on a custom design for a pair of antique doors from India, which we used as a headboard in a bedroom design (see page 195).

Go room by room through your home and see what you can fix without spending much. Ask yourself if you really need to rip out all the cabinets in the kitchen because they're dated or if it's just the color or the wood finish that's the problem. If you paint the kitchen yourself, it will look completely different. Decide what is working, what can stay and be reworked, and what needs to be replaced. Try to problem-solve investing in big changes.

Thrifting 101

I've said it before, and I'll say it again: I'm a thrifter. I love to find items that have a worn, lived-in look while still bringing a unique sophistication to a room. A found object can elevate a space perfectly without feeling fussy or overdone. Here's my best advice for hunting down finds:

- **Don't overthink it.** Dumb it down when you are thrifting, especially if you are shopping online, like on Facebook Marketplace or Craigslist. It may feel overwhelming, because for every great piece, there are twenty you'd never spend time on. But there are some fantastic bargains to be found on these sites. Hold your cards close to your chest and keep your opinions about the product, such as worth or designer, to yourself. The more you disclose to the seller, the more you are hurting your chances of bargaining for a better price. For example, if I'm looking for a mid-century modern sofa, I change my verbiage to be as simple as possible, such as by referring to it as a couch, and avoid "designer" words. The key is to act like the seller doesn't know what they have and as if you don't know what they have, either.

- **Be open.** Often, when you go to a thrift shop or a flea market, you are looking for a very specific thing, but then you walk out with items that you didn't necessarily know you were going to find. I have found so many great, unexpected things by keeping an open mind. Sometimes the bargains are too good to walk away from.

- **Play it cool.** Don't let on to the vendor that you are excited when you see a piece you know you are walking out with. This will hurt your ability to haggle.

- **As we all learned from *Project Runway*, you're either in, or you're out.** When thrifting, you need to be all in, 150 percent, or pass on the item entirely. You need to really love the piece. If you're on the fence, don't buy it. You need to love it before you leave the store, or it's just going to gather dust, sitting at the back of a closet. Be open and intentional when making your purchases.

As an aside, please do your due diligence when buying online through secondhand buyers to protect yourself and make sure you aren't being scammed.

- **Look at everything before making any decisions.** When at an antiques store, a thrift shop, or a flea market, take your time and walk through all the booths or aisles before purchasing anything. While at an estate sale, you might have to move a bit quicker; pick up things and edit your haul later. The same goes for when you are in a place with a cart. Set your pace based on the crowd, fill your cart, and edit at the end. Now, obviously, if you find something that is just an unbelievable bargain, then scoop it up, no matter what!

- **Always haggle.** It doesn't matter what they tell you is their lowest price. Haggle anyway, and be prepared to walk away. Ask the person selling the item, such as at a flea market, vintage store, estate sale, swap meet, or antiques market or online, what their best price is, and then negotiate from there. If someone knows the value of what they have, it will be more difficult to haggle, but maybe they've been holding on to the item for a long time and are ready to move it regardless of the value, or maybe they are just feeling generous. Either way, it never hurts to ask. Another approach is the bundle effect. If you see several things that you like from one vendor, then see if you can negotiate a set price. For example, if I'm interested in three items or five items for a total of $170 but really only want to spend $120, I will ask the vendor if they can do all the items for $100. This gives the vendor wiggle room to counter with another price, such as $120, saving you $50. Always offer less than you want to spend so you have time to get to the sweet spot where you feel comfortable. You've got this. Go get those deals.

- **Always have cash.** You're going to be able to make out a lot better if you have cash because vendors will be more willing to offer deals on the objects you are interested in purchasing.

- **Do your research.** Check the bottom of a vase or a bowl. Know what real crystal looks like and some of the names that you might find on a piece. Know where things are made and when things stopped being produced somewhere. Snap a picture of the item and do a quick search online to see if you can find the value of a piece. Lift the seat cushions and see which manufacturer made the item. Really study the pieces at hand to see how the vendor's price compares to the value.

- **Come prepared.** Don't leave home without a measuring tape. Also measure certain areas of your home so you know exactly what will fit where. I know I said to be open, but if you are looking for a very specific thing, go ahead and measure your space. And I would encourage you to save those dimensions so when you're out, you can measure items just to make sure they will fit in your space. Take photos and save them to your phone.

- **Use an app-driven delivery service for convenience.** There are so many app-driven delivery services. If you are in a big city, many of them will pick up the item from the vendor and bring it into your home for you.

EAT DRINK NAP

JAKE ARNOLD

TIPS FOR CREATING FLAWLESS ART PAIRINGS

- Pair a color photo with an abstract painting that shares a color with the image.
- Pair a neutral abstract with a sketch or a muted landscape.
- Pair a vintage realist painting with a black-and-white photo.
- Coordinate the artwork's color, style, and texture with the textures of your space, pulling elements of the room into the art you place in the space.
- Look for prints if the original is unavailable or out of budget.
- When in doubt, turn to social media. Reach out directly to an artist and inquire about buying art from them directly. You can find great pieces from artists not yet showing in galleries and purchase art for a fraction of the price. This route allows you to see work pairings to balance your room effortlessly.

HOW TO GET THE LOOK

- Layer square or rectangular framed art to lean against the wall on the left or right.
- Hang a round mirror or a larger abstract piece of art to the right. The circle will break up the squares and rectangles of the art to the left. This will give your eyes somewhere to rest as your gaze moves across the mantel.
- Treat the mantel like a mini coffee table and bring in neutral books and a plant, a vase, or an object to stack in front of the art leaning on or hanging above the mantel. This will give height and texture to the layers.

Scaling Artwork

Select art that makes a statement within your home—the bigger the canvas, the better, I say. A large canvas means less clutter and less to build within the room. When you go too small, you run the risk of the balance being thrown off. If you already have a lot of pieces, this is the time to build a gallery wall. A tapestry could also be used as a large piece of art behind a sofa or a bed.

SMOKE AND MIRRORS

I want to let you in on a secret—many high-end and big-box stores are sourcing art from the same places. For example, you can find printable artwork on Etsy for about $5. This is the same artwork that you will find in several stores. Once an artist releases their work to be used, unless they have an exclusive contract, it can be sold in many locations. This is a great way to get inexpensive artwork. Just purchase, print, and frame.

For every modern piece, add something traditional and vice versa. Here you'll see that mix in play: (*above*) we hung a modern piece below a traditional painting. And (*opposite*) we hung a mid-century modern piece in a Victorian home.

Styling and Layering Like a Champ

"How do you do that?" is the number one question I get asked, and it doesn't matter if I'm on set or walking down the street. You all want to know how I style my looks, whether it's a coffee table, a bookcase, an armoire, or even just the pillows on a bed.

So let's break down my favorite tricks for all your styling needs.

Opposite: Layering objects found in most kitchens, like wooden spoons in a neutral vessel and a stack of cookbooks, is a quick way to add warmth to a room. Mixing the different tones of color makes for a nice moment.

CALL IT HOME

AMBER LEWIS

POTTER

MAGNOLIA TABLE

JOANNA GAINES

wm
MORROW

Magnolia Table

VOLUME I

JOANNA GAINES

wm
MORROW

Magnolia Table

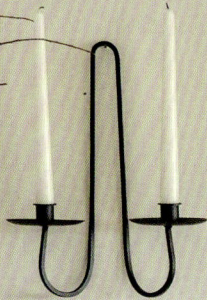

Pick books that work with the room aesthetically. I'm not talking about grabbing books off the shelf just because you like the *subject* of the book. Honey, we are here to judge all the books by their covers. Pause and think about what you are going to select. Remember, these books are going to be on display as part of your design and story, so pick well and pick wisely.

The Star of the Show: The Coffee Table

Let's start with the item that I receive the most requests for help with: the coffee table.

First, gather pieces that speak to you to display on the table, then pull out the larger items. (You can set the smaller items aside for now. We will get to them.) The more oversized items will be the foundational pieces in this beautiful look you are creating.

When styling a coffee table, I love to use books. Don't sleep on this tip—books will go a long way in your design. Look for large-scale books that can carry the table's weight and add height to give you that wow moment as you begin to stack and layer. Then you can place objects next to and on top of the books to help tell your story through styling.

Remember, this is part of your story, and you want the objects to be part of your home in an effortless way. Embrace the art of the nestle, too—add one or two tiny things into the design, so it all feels cohesive and related. A small cluster of items on the coffee table and on the mantel creates a nice layer of repetition and illusion that they are worth more than they are. For example, use two small bowls or saucers with neutral, wood decorative beads draped over the edge to step up the look a bit.

Opposite: Allow the coffee table to be a statement piece in your home. Maybe it stands out because of its architectural features or a beautiful woodgrain. What you display on top of the table is equally important.

SMOKE AND MIRRORS

On *Hack My Home,* we often don't have the rights to feature an item, which is why you sometimes see artwork, T-shirts, or books blurred out. Once, while filming an episode, we needed a lot of books. So instead of getting licensing from every author, we went to the dollar store and thrift shops and found books, removed the dust jackets, and then turned the books around so all you saw were the bound pages of the books. This move turns your books almost into an art installation, with the creaminess of the pages, in different tones, lining your shelves. Now, you don't have to worry about licensing in your home, but this look neutralizes a space. If you don't want to turn your books around, just remove the dust jackets of the hardbound books to take away some of the busyness of the spines. Sometimes you want to be surrounded by books, but the neon green of one of the spines isn't working with the overall aesthetics of the space. This is a great trick when you are faced with that.

Do Go Chasing Waterfalls

Let's discuss the "waterfall effect" and how to use this design secret in your styling. This approach will give you that cascading feeling, much like a waterfall with the highest peak, the natural middle portion, and then the bottom, where all the water collects. You want to style with this in mind, giving your eyes a smooth transition as they move from one group to the next, never having to ask, "Where do my eyes need to land?" Stay away from drastic highs and lows.

Opposite: A side table deserves a "waterfall effect" styling moment. It's a small surface that lends itself to grouping in threes.

ARRANGING THINGS

KARL LAGERFELD   A LINE OF BEAUTY

ANDY WARHOL
Polaroids 1958–1987

Hilma af Klint - The Paintings for the Temple 1906–1915

When you have a larger coffee table in a big room, think about counterbalance. If you have your three groups—high, middle, and low—on one side of the coffee table, quiet the look with two simple stacks of neutral books on the other side.

Once you have the high, middle, and low objects that speak to you and the room's aesthetics, you want to make sure your middle object is about half the height of the high item. Going too tall will throw off the balance of the table.

Opposite and above: Placed atop books for height and added interest, these sculptures have more of a presence in their respective rooms.

STYLING IN GROUPS OF THREE

- **High**—consider something such as a tall vase or a sculptural piece.

- **Middle**—look for books to stack.

- **Low**—choose items to layer on top of the middle grouping, such as a bowl, a small box, or a small plant.

I'm a fan of creating collections through color, so in my design projects, I like to find books with the shades we need to tie the space together. Look around your space and think about what you can pull from other areas of the room to draw your eyes to the coffee table. Now step back and evaluate the scale of the items on the table.

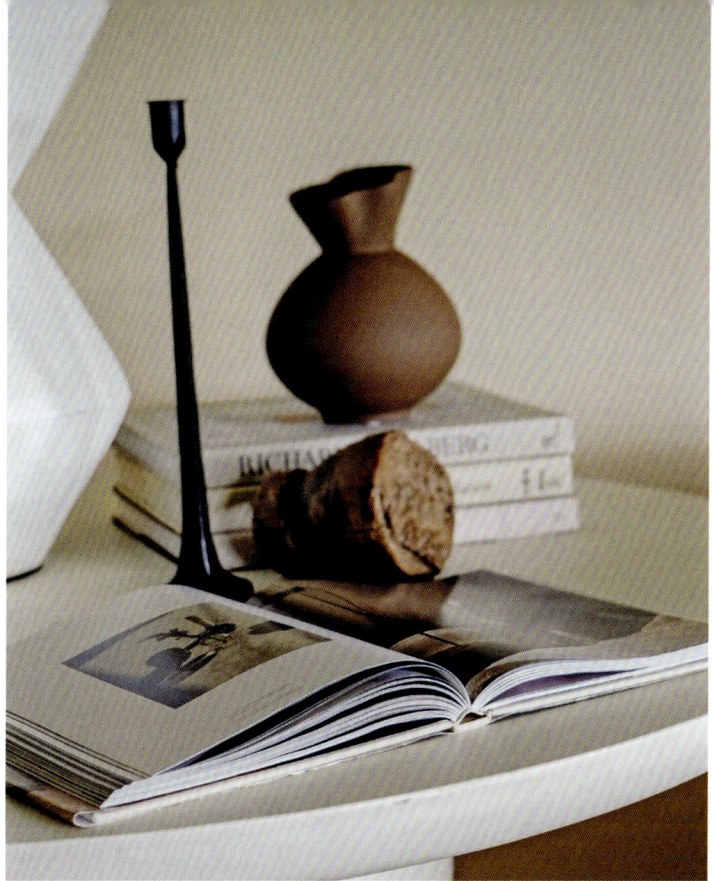

If you decide to use a sculptural piece for your high item, be bold and choose a piece that has meaning for you: something from your culture, a vintage or repurposed item, or an artistic work that ties the room together, such as a piece you make yourself using found objects.

Opposite and above: Whether on mantels, side tables, or dining tables, vases work as both sculptural art and a useful way to display cut branches or fresh flowers.

Tiny Real Estate

Mantels can be tricky to style based on how deep or wide they are. You can go the toned-down, minimal route and place just one item on your mantel. I take this approach quite frequently, and that's okay! If a single item is your speed, choose one that's about half the width of the mantel. This could be a large-scale mirror or a piece of art. Let's do some math. If your mantel is 100 inches long, you will want to ensure that the one significant-sized item you select is between 50 and 65 inches.

Layered Styling

Honey, you didn't pick up this book for basic, easy design 101, so let's dive into the layers you can bring to the space with this narrow bit of real estate. Again, you will work with the idea of the waterfall effect, much like you did with the coffee table.

Start with a larger piece of art on the left, and style to the right by layering a smaller piece of framed art next to it, leaning it against the wall. Make sure the two pieces of art work well together. They aren't twins—not even fraternal ones—but they are related, and you want to see that they share a grandmother.

Power Clashing Our Art

Even if you've never heard the term "power clashing," you've probably seen it. Power clashing is when two contrasting patterns are paired to create a cohesive look, and it applies when art pieces that wouldn't typically be paired look surprisingly great when placed side by side. If you aren't familiar with selecting art or don't know how to look for it, finding the art that works best in your home might initially feel like a foreign concept. You will be a natural once you become more comfortable mixing and matching. Think of it like pairing clothing. We know what works well together and feels good to us as we discover our own style. Picking art is much the same. It becomes part of our story. If you find a floral painting you love, think about how you can mix it with a photograph that has some of the same colors. It's not a direct match, but they go together naturally. The same goes for picking paint for our homes. You know what works well together and which colors you love. With much going on, an abstract painting can be toned down with a black-and-white sketch. You can move pieces around until you feel like you have the correct pairings. If you want a more uniform look to your art, consider putting all the pieces in the same frame or in slight variations of the same frame. Or select a mix of abstract and realist paintings in the same color family, then mix in some black-and-white sketches and black-and-white photographs to create a cohesive collection.

Opposite: Sometimes you don't need a lot of accessories—one statement piece can hold its own.

We had fun finding an artful chair to mimic this large oversized piece on the wall. Placing the chair off-center to the art draws the eye in for a nice asymmetrical moment.

Function meets form in this sitting area, which is part of an office, that I designed to feel like a cozy living room.

- Group items that share a linear form.
- Stick to a limited colorway.
- Look for items of the same height and texture.

Styling a Bookshelf Is My Love Language

Finally, I would love, love, love to help you all with your bookshelves. While they are meant to hold books, that's not their only job. I want to help you reclaim your shelves and bring them into your story.

When you are styling a bookshelf, it's really going to come down to how you display things you love aesthetically.

The first thing you want to be aware of is item placement. When I look at a bookshelf, I think of it as a single unit. And I want my ideas to have balance. So how do we accomplish that?

Treat every other shelf the same, meaning the top shelf will have the same balance and flow as the third shelf, fifth shelf, and so on.

For example, if you have a grouping of objects, such as pottery or wood vessels, on the top shelf, on the third shelf, you might place an object such as a woven basket, to bring in a soft, natural touch. Treat the even-numbered shelves with the waterfall effect and cluster items using the principles of high, middle, and low. This time, unlike when styling the coffee table and the mantel, you should add more clusters if space allows.

- Using odd numbers, start with three clusters, then move to five or seven as you work across the shelf, depending on its length.

- Use a tray as your high item, leaning it against the back of the bookshelf, then cluster a double stack of wood bowls next to a taller vessel.

- Jumping down to the next empty shelf, you will want to bring in other shapes to break up the round items—use a stack of books lying flat with an item on top to create one cluster. A framed work of art behind the books will act as the high item.

- A round basket with thoughtfully selected items inside completes the look.

This is a type of reverse symmetry in which the shelves match and work together, yet you want to avoid making the composition obvious. Subliminal styling at its best.

Opposite: Bookshelves don't have to hold just books! In fact, I love to tell a story using my favorite objects. It creates a "china cabinet" moment, but in a more modern way.

SMOKE AND MIRRORS

You can change up the art pairings occasionally by moving art around, leaning art on the mantel rather than hanging it on the wall, or switching art out to create a seasonal look to your decor. It's a simple trick to give you a subtle refresh.

High Ceilings, High Styling

When you have higher ceilings, lower bookshelves, or even longer walls, you can break them up with a console table and objects that might give you more height, such as a plant or a large piece of art. Here are some suggestions:

- Look for an oversized piece of art to provide drama and fill the space.

- Draw the eye up slightly but not too high.

- Anchor the space with a large piece of art that won't compete with the groupings.

- Look for a large plant that will hit above the art, continuing with the waterfall effect again.

- Treat the console table as one of your clusters, balancing the arrangement. Placing other clusters alongside the plant and in front of the painting creates the effect you want when styling a large room.

- Remember to account for scale. Larger, wider objects balance the room.

When styling, one final design rule is to work in odd numbers and group in pairs of three, five, or seven. A stack of books with a bowl on top is one group, while a large vase with greenery is another. Each group is a unit. You can break this rule if you have a larger surface and use an even number of groupings to balance the overall look.

Opposite: Add visual height to a desk or table by placing a large vessel and a couple of cheap and cheerful branches to draw the eye upward, which will create more optical variety in the room.

RESOURCES

LEGEND

A—Artwork
B—Bath & body
C—Candles & fragrance
D—Decor
DH—Decorative hardware
F—Furniture
K—Kitchen
L—Lighting
P—Paint
R—Rugs
S&T—Stone & tile
T—Textiles & fabric
V—Vintage items
W—Wallpaper
WC—Window coverings

A

ABC CARPET & HOME / abchome.com / New York, New York

F/D/R/L/A/C/DH/K

This NYC staple has an entire basement level dedicated to rugs. It also has a restaurant called ABC Kitchen that has won several culinary awards. So shop, have lunch, and then shop some more.

AERO / aerostudios.com / New York, New York

F/D/L/A

Aero is a great showroom with a wide range of furniture and lighting. The brown leather chair in my Kips Bay Decorator Show House bedroom is from them.

ALLMODERN / allmodern.com / various locations

F/D/L/R/A/C/DH/ WC/K

I've used this online shop for several TV makeovers and residential projects. I love its quick-ship options, which take less than a week.

ANTHROPOLOGIE / anthropologie.com / various locations

F/D/L/R/A/C/DH/WC/K

Although this is a clothing store, it also has great furniture and decor. I've scored several limited-edition pieces because Anthropologie often partners with prominent designers to create capsule collections.

ARHAUS / arhaus.com / various locations

F/D/L/R/A/C/DH/B/T/WC/K

This is one of my go-to resources when sourcing for clients. I love that the showrooms offer several items with an aged patina that look like real vintage furniture.

B

BENJAMIN MOORE / benjaminmoore.com / various locations

P

This is one of my go-to resources for paint because I know the finish will be consistent. I use Benjamin Moore paint extensively on television because it typically dries quicker than other brands. I love that they also have large swatches and not the tiny ones that you usually find in paint stores.

C

CB2 / cb2.com / various locations

F/D/L/R/A/V/W/C/DH/WC/K

This furniture store played an important role in my life. While working at CB2, I met a set designer who worked with Emily Henderson and got a job as an intern on her TV show. Besides that, this is an amazing source for high-end pieces without the hefty designer price tag.

CHASING PAPER / chasingpaper.com

W

This is one of the first companies to offer peel-and-stick wallpaper. I've used it on several TV shows, including *The Steve Harvey Show*. The owner, Elizabeth Rees, even sent her sister Annie to help me install the paper for my first segment. This product is great for renters or commitmentphobes.

CLARE / clare.com

P

This is one of my favorite paint stores because of the strong, saturated tones they have created. Fun fact: Nicole Gibbons, the owner, and I both grew up in the same city. I went to middle school with her sister. This is also a Black-owned business.

+COOP / Los Angeles, California

F/D/L/R/A/V/C

This is an excellent resource for hard-to-find pieces that will give your home a genuine wow factor. Nothing in this store is cookie-cutter.

COSENTINO / cosentino.com

S&T

I can't say enough about this brand! They are the leader in stainable stone for indoor and outdoor design. I use their stone on countertops, outdoors, on walls, and more. Plus, their VP of Architect and Design Sales, Patty Dominguez, is a complete sweetheart who treats you like family whenever you see her!

COUP D'ETAT / coupdetatsf.com / Los Angeles and San Francisco, California

F/D/L/R/A/V/C

This is another great source for items that make you pause, the type of items that you would see in a magazine.

COWSHED INTERIORS / cowshed.com

B/C

This is a British-based spa under the Soho House umbrella. Their full line of shower gels is provided in every hotel room, and this is how I found out about the brand. Their gray hooded bathrobe is my life! It is supersoft, and I even have two robes so I can keep one on while the other is in the wash.

COWTAN & TOUT / cowtan.com / various locations

F/W

If you love floral fabrics, you are in luck! Cowtan & Tout reigns supreme in the design world when it comes to great printed fabrics. But don't sleep on their solids as well. My favorite is Manuel Canovas's collection.

CRATE & BARREL / crateandbarrel.com / various locations

F/D/L/R/A/V/W/C/DH/WC/K

This store is where I first fell in love with design. I often tell the story of how I was working at Bloomingdale's and found myself in Crate & Barrel at Perimeter Mall in Atlanta, Georgia, while on my lunch break. When I looked up, I had spent forty minutes of my forty-five-minute break in the store and didn't have time to grab lunch. That was the day I knew I wanted to pursue a career in interior design.

CURREY & COMPANY / curreyandcompany.com / various locations

F/D/L/A

This is a great brand that several retailers carry in their stores. You can now shop directly from the source, making it easier and cheaper!

D

THE DESIGN HOUSE BY HDC / heuerdesigncollective.com

F/D/L/R/A/C/T/B/V/K

I am a bit partial to this store because my friend Dawn Heuer created its concept. She is known for her English Cotswolds—inspired designs, which make it a favorite of mine. When it comes to working with color and pattern, she literally provides the road map to success. Walk the salesroom floor several times and take in as much design inspiration as possible.

DONALDSON FINE ART / amydonaldson.com / various galleries and online

A

Amy Donaldson is an amazing artist who creates unique abstract pieces using paint mixed with sand and ground-up shrimp shells. My Kips Bay Decorator Show House room features her work.

E

ETHAN ALLEN / ethanallen.com / various locations

F/D/L/R/A/WC/K

These stores are a great resource for timeless classics with a modern twist. Fun fact: Ethan Allen is one of the few approved vendors for the White House. I learned this when I submitted a bid to design a room within the White House.

THE EXPERT / theexpert.com

F/D/A/L/T/V

This platform allows you to book thirty- or sixty-minute design consultations with some of your favorite interior designers (shameless plug: you can also book a session with me here). And now the site has an online section that allows you to purchase several items curated by the designers. They also have a new brick-and-mortar location where you can view vintage items.

F

FARROW & BALL / farrow-ball.com/us / various locations

P/W

This is one of the best brands for high-end paint finishes. It is a UK-based company that offers very sophisticated colors with rich tones. There was even a spoof on *SNL* about the high quality of their paint.

FIRECLAY TILE / fireclaytile.com / various locations

S&T

I came across this brand while working on my bathroom at Real Simple Home. I love their selection of glazed and matte tiles. They even have several quick-ship options to get things out in a week. Best of all, they offer installation as well.

14TH STREET MODERN & VINTAGE HOME / 14thstreetantiques.com / Atlanta, Georgia

F/D/L/A/V

They have a secret floor downstairs where a lot of merchandise that hasn't made it to the sales floor is stored. If you are nice to the sales rep, they may give you a sneak peek.

G

THE GOLDEN TRIANGLE /
goldentriangle.biz / Chicago, Illinois

F/D/L/R/A/V

This is one of my top shops for sourcing antiques. Doug Van Tress and Chauwarin Tuntisak, the owners, take frequent trips to India and Asia to source products. They even have a portion of an Indian mansion that was deconstructed and rebuilt in the showroom. It looks like a real home when you step into this showroom. They also have cool events, like performances by a small chamber ensemble. They've made custom pieces for me based on drawings that I've done on a napkin. Doug is amazing! Ask for him.

H

HD BUTTERCUP / hdbuttercup.com /
Los Angeles, California

F/D/L/R/A/V/DH/K

This is a Los Angeles staple! Several vendors in this warehouse space carry items ranging from super bargains to high-end pieces. I learned about this store while filming HGTV *Design Star* (season 7). We shopped here for episode 3.

HOUSE OF HACKNEY /
us.houseofhackney.com

W/T/WC

I love their bold use of patterns in a tasteful English manner. They are known for their tapestries, scenic wallpaper, and trims. They even have matching fabrics and wallpapers to help you coordinate spaces with ease.

HUDSON VALLEY LIGHTING /
hvlgroup.com / various locations

L

This is an excellent resource for interesting lighting. It houses several prominent interior designers' collections, with quick-ship options. This is one of the showrooms that sells its items to larger stores, so you can often find better deals by shopping here directly.

I

INCOLLECT / incollect.com

F/D/L/R/A/V/C/DH

This is a hidden gem in NYC. Their in-person showroom is a conglomerate of high-end design shops all under one roof! Best of all, it is open to the public, and people don't really know because it's located inside 200 Lex, which is geared toward the trade. They even have an online site, so you don't have to leave your home to shop. The sales team is very friendly and doesn't have a pretentious vibe. I hope to have a booth in this showroom someday soon!

J

JAYSON HOME / jaysonhome.com /
various locations

F/D/L/R/A/V/C/B/T/DH/K

This store is my primary go-to when sourcing rare finds. The showroom is set up like a two-story home with an entire area devoted to vintage items, plus an outdoor garden area. From furniture to kitchen and bath items, they have it all! Their products are featured in just about every project in my book. They even did a pop-up shop with the Bergdorf Goodman department store.

JEAN DE MERRY / demerry.com

F/D/L/R/A

This is the holy grail of modern luxury design. If you want striking pieces that no one else will have, look no further. My favorite find was a hand-painted glass artwork that required three installers to remove sixty individually painted glass panels.

JONATHAN ADLER /
jonathanadler.com /
various locations

F/D/L/R/A/V/C/B/K

If mid-century modern is your jam, this store won't let you down. I've been shopping here for years. Once I began designing for clients, it was one of the first stores I wanted to work with. They are also known for their quirky pottery and statement needlepoint pillows with phrases that would shock Grandma!

JUNIPER & BROS. /
etsy.com/shop/JuniperandBros /
Etsy shop

F

Sometimes you accidentally stumble upon something so good that you don't want to share it with anyone. If I had to gatekeep, this would be my place. Jessica and Kurt Schleinz make vintage replicas of beautiful bespoke wood items. If you think of it, they can probably make it! You will see several of their custom-carved pieces throughout *Forever Home*.

JUSTCO / shopjustco.com /
Miami, Florida

F/D/L/R/A/V/C

Even as a designer, I would let the owner of this shop, Briggs Solomon, design my house! The showroom is in a warehouse, yet it doesn't feel cold or sterile. All the products are vintage items that have been restored or reupholstered. The wood pieces that they've collected are the star of the show. They have worked with celebs like A-Rod and more.

K

KARL KEMP ANTIQUES / karlkemp.com / New York, New York

F/D/L/A/V

I came across this shop while walking down the street in NYC. The moodily lit storefront lures you in. They have a ton of perfectly curated vignettes and items you'll want to put on your wish list.

KATHY KUO HOME / kathykuohome.com

F/D/L/R/A/V/C/B/K

Whenever I search for beautiful modern pieces online, this showroom appears on my feed—and I'm certainly grateful for it! Their prices are reasonable, and I can also find solid items that don't look like everyone else's.

KOHLER / kohler.com / various locations

L/K/B/DH

Kohler is a brand that combines innovation and timeless design, making it a go-to for quality kitchen and bath products. Fun fact: after I was seated next to David Kohler at a gala, he took the time to send me the nicest handwritten letter! It really highlights the brand's commitment to personal connections and exceptional customer service.

KRAVET / kravet.com / various locations

F/D/L/R/A/T/W/WC

This is undoubtedly one of the powerhouses for fabric, textiles, wallpaper, trim, and furniture. Their catalog of products is beyond impressive. Whether you're looking for outdoor performance fabric for your patio or a chic upholstery updated

for a family heirloom, they've got you covered!

L

LAUREL MERCANTILE / laurelmercantile.com / Laurel, Mississippi

F/D/L/R/A/V/C/B/K

This shop is the brainchild of HGTV stars Erin and Ben Napier. Walking in transports you back to when life was simple. A whirl around the shop is excellent for nostalgia alone! They have everything from hand-carved kitchen goods to candles, accessories, and clothing.

LAWTON MULL / lawtonmull.com / New York, New York

F/D/L/R/A/V

Shearling sofa . . . those two words say it all! I fell in love with this showroom when I came across their hand-carved Otto Wretling wood sofa that had been reupholstered in shearling wool. You can see this piece in my Kips Bay Decorator Show House bedroom design. Cordelia Lawton and Patrick Mull own this shop curated with various jaw-dropping vintage items. Every corner will leave you in awe.

LE LABO / lelabofragrances.com / various locations

C/B

This is the cult classic for candles and scents. I first learned of Le Labo and the infamous Santal 26 candle scent permeating a hotel lobby in Chicago in 2014. When I visited the shop, I fell in love with the deconstructed and rustic feel of it. They even make cologne, which I use as a room scent. The sales rep makes your scent like a chemist right in front of you and creates a custom-printed label on-site. Pro tip: save your empty bottle and return it for a refill discount. My favorite candles and colognes are Santal 26,

Another 13, and Thé Matcha 26. They coordinate candles for several cologne scents, and they are all unisex.

LEE JOFA / kravet.com/lee-jofa / various locations

T/W/F/WC

I am obsessed with their high-end fabric, trims, and wallpaper. They have several timeless classics and modern patterns that can be used throughout the home. I feature quite a few of their fabrics in the book.

LOLOI RUGS

A/D/R/T

I discovered Loloi Rugs while sourcing rugs for the set design of *The Steve Harvey Show*. Renowned for their stunning rug collections, textiles, and artwork, they collaborate with top designers like Amber Lewis, Joanna Gaines, and Brigette Romanek, offering unique stylish pieces for any space.

LONE FOX / lonefox.com

F/D/L/R/A/C/T/B/V/K

The failed gatekeeper strikes again! I'm having difficulty writing this out, but I must share it with the world. Drew Michael Scott, aka Lone Fox, is huge on social media due to his jaw-dropping DIY makeovers. (Do yourself a favor and look him up right now.) He now has a retail shop with many vintage curiosities and modern decor items.

M

MAGNOLIA HOME / magnolia.com / Waco, Texas

F/D/L/R/A/V/C/B/WC/K

There's no question that Joanna Gaines is the Queen of Interior Design for our generation. So of course her store is filled with a slew of beautiful and practical items to complete your home. Fun fact: in 2020, Joanna contacted me on

Instagram. So I made a funny video saying, "Now that I've met Joanna Gaines, I can die and go see Jesus." She then reached out to me about doing a show! I appeared on *Design Defined* on Magnolia Network.

MAIDEN HOME / maidenhome.com / New York, New York

F/D/L/R/A/V/C

This is another design gem that I'm so glad I stumbled upon during an internet search. Their designs are minimal yet thought-provoking. I would say they are the perfect example of quiet luxury.

MAISON GERARD / maisongerard.com / New York, New York

F/D/L/A/V

If you're into small, standout decorative moments, this is your place! They have many accessories and small case goods that scream "Look at me!" without being gaudy. Take your time in this showroom and walk the floor a few times. You'll find something interesting that you missed each time. Pro tip: they have a second location a few doors down.

MANZILI BY HUDA / manzilibyhuda.com

A

There's a reason why Crate & Barrel collaborated with Huda Hashim. Her work is stunning! I love her effortless brushstrokes that seem to create abstract masterpieces. She also does commission work if you want something a little more bespoke.

MARRS MERCANTILE / marrsmercantile.com / Centerton, Arkansas

F/D/L/R/A/V/C/B/K

We all have a super-supportive social media friend that we've never met

in person. For me, it's HGTV star Jenny Marrs! To top it off, she and her husband, Dave Marrs, have a fantastic store with several products that will refresh your home.

MCGEE & CO. / mcgeeandco.com

F/D/L/R/A/V/C/B/DH/WC/K

If you love home decor, this brand should be a no-brainer! Shea and Syd McGee have taken the design world by storm with their casual yet sophisticated aesthetic. Anything that they carry will be tasteful. Their items are also great if you want to introduce color into your home but don't know where to start. Fun fact: Shea wrote a foreword for this book, and I wrote the foreword for her first book, *Make Life Beautiful*.

MEODED PAINT & PLASTER / meodedpaint.com / Los Angeles, California

P

This is my go-to resource for limewash or textured walls. They have many great color options and will even send you large test swatches before you commit.

MICHAEL DEL PIERO GOOD DESIGN / michaeldelpiero.com / Chicago, Illinois

F/D/L/R/A/V/C

I have been a fan of Michael Del Piero's for years! She is secretly a mentor, even though she doesn't know it. I've long studied her tasteful design. All of her products are neutral but never boring. Each piece will tell a story. Whether it's an intricately carved wooden chair from Africa or a raw-edge stone vessel, you can guarantee that anything you purchase in this shop will be unique.

MINTED / minted.com

A/D

I often use Minted on my television makeovers because they have great

artwork that can be matted and framed with a push of a button on their site. They've even added one-of-a-kind pieces curated by local artisans.

MONTAUK SOFA / montauksofa.com / various locations

F/D/A

My first high-end sofa for a project came from this showroom. My go-to is the Chicago location; the store literally looks like a modern loft home that is ready for you to move right into. I love their take on classic design with a subtle modern twist. Also, give their art and accessories a peek. Nothing in this store will disappoint!

N

NEWEL / newel.com / New York, New York / Hollywood, Florida

F/D/L/R/A/V

Think of a warehouse the size of Home Depot, then double it! That's exactly how large their loft showroom feels. There are rows and rows of antiques, artwork, furniture, and oversized decor pieces. The store is highly organized and offers rentals for designers and set decorators. Fun fact: they frequently rent to several big TV productions, including *Saturday Night Live*.

O

OLIVE ATELIERS / oliveateliers.com / Los Angeles, California

F/D/L/R/A/V/K

One look at their website, and you will want to book a flight to Los Angeles. This is the home of perfectly imperfect objects. They specialize in hand-chiseled wood and stone items. The showroom is open only on specific days at specific times, and they have crazy-long lines of eager shoppers. Pro tip: you can shop online by signing up for their "Drop" announcement to see when items go on sale (typically the day after the in-person sale). But act fast because items sell quickly as soon as they are dropped.

P

POOKY LIGHTING / us.pooky.com

L/D

This is one of my favorite resources for good-looking cordless lighting. They even have wireless wall sconces! I am also a massive fan of their decor items.

PORTMANTEAU / portmanteaunewyork.com / New York, New York

F/D/V

Another one of my vintage sources that I would prefer to gatekeep! The shop is run by appointment only, so you can enjoy a relaxed shopping experience. If you shop vintage, you know this is rare. They also have online shopping.

POTTERY BARN / potterybarn.com / various locations

F/D/L/R/A/V/W/C/DH/B/WC/K

If nothing else, you can always count on this store for timeless classics that will last. I use their products for many of my television makeovers because they typically have items in stock. I love how they also have small in-store pop-up shops that feature local artists.

PRESTON KONRAD / prestonkonrad.com / New York, New York

F/D/L/R/A/V/W/C/B/K

When it comes to up-and-coming design, Preston Konrad is always a leader of the pack. He is an interior designer and style expert who recently opened a brick-and-mortar location in NYC. He has several great statement decor items, his own line of candles, and even a chic luxury home-care line

with household cleaners and hand soaps. If you appreciate details, you will admire the sophisticated packaging that will blend in with the rest of your home.

R

REJUVENATION / rejuvenation.com / various locations

F/D/L/R/V/W/C/H/DH

Initially, I discovered this brand while shopping on an episode of *Design Star*. Known for their fantastic lighting options, they have since turned into a design powerhouse with furniture and rugs. Pro tip: they have stunning cabinet hardware. Upgrade your builder's basic cabinets with their interesting assortment of knobs and drawer pulls.

RESSOURCE / ressourcepaints.us / New York, New York

P/W

I have an iconic Instagram photo of a navy blue bookcase. Well, folks, this is where the paint for the project came from. I am a huge fan of their saturated tones and textured paint. They have large swatches on thick cardstock, which is a huge bonus!

RH / rh.com / various locations

F/D/L/R/V/W/C/H/DH/B/WC/K

Any retail store that doesn't need social media must be doing something right. This showroom is essentially a walking design bible. I constantly come here to reference their seating configurations for projects. Pro tip: several locations have a restaurant inside the store, and the food is always excellent!

THE RILEY/LAND COLLECTION / riley-land.com / Smyrna, Tennessee

F/D/L/R/A/V/C/B/DH//K

Once again, I'm terrible at gatekeeping. This is one of the most under-the-radar shops that I frequent. They are known for kitchenware and hand-carved wooden goods, but it's a little-known fact that they carry furniture and accessories as well. Pro tip: I know this is a decor book, but they have a monthly gourmet mystery box subscription for even the most discerning foodies.

ROMAN AND WILLIAMS GUILD / rwguild.com / New York, New York

F/D/L/R/A/V/C/B/K

This is another showroom that can have the keys to my home and free rein to redesign anything as they see fit. The showroom has a variety of high-end furniture and decor items. They also have a great restaurant that looks like a Parisian café. Fun fact: the principals of this design house, Robin Standefer and Stephen Alesch, are a famous duo known for their work with several commercial spaces, and they designed the set for *The Drew Barrymore Show*.

ROMO / romo.com / various locations

T/W/WC

This brand has gotten more business from me than any other fabric showroom. Their colorways and fabrics are refined, and several of my projects throughout the book feature them.

ROOM & BOARD / roomandboard.com / various locations

F/D/L/R/V/W/C/H/DH

This store is for all mid-century design lovers. The quality of their products is impeccable as well. I have a client who purchased a sofa from them more than ten years ago, and it still looks new! Pro tip: they occasionally sell vintage items in a bazaar-like pop-up shop where you can grab items from around the world.

S

SCHUMACHER / schumacher.com / various locations

T/W/WC

This brand has a large array of high-end fabrics, wallpaper, and trim. It is sold to the trade only, but you can find several of their products online. Pro tip: several "trade only" brands can be found on sites like Etsy, where designers offer pillows, drapes, and other items made from fabric they've purchased.

SEMIHANDMADE / semihandmade.com

F/DH/K

The brand is the hack of all hacks! Picture this . . . you go to IKEA, purchase basic cabinet bases, and then add Semihandmade door fronts. Their products instantly upgrade most IKEA cabinetry units. They have a custom line of cabinetry as well.

SERENA & LILY / serenaandlily.com / various locations

F/D/L/R/A/C/T/B/WC/K

Do yourself a favor and visit a city that has a Serena & Lily showroom. The products typically lean more coastal, but not in a cheesy beach-word-art type of way. Think more refined rattan and seersucker.

THE SHADE STORE / theshadestore.com / various locations

WC

Without question, this store is the

leader when it comes to custom drapery. From start to finish, they do all the legwork. The showroom has drawers full of drapery fabrics for various needs. The sales rep will help you select the best options for your space and send a team to template your order. A few weeks later, they install and steam everything for you. It doesn't get much more manageable.

SHERWIN-WILLIAMS / sherwin-williams.com / various locations

P/W

This paint brand is synonymous with excellent quality. They have a vast color selection, and you can always count on their color of the year to be trendsetting. Pro tip: they've partnered with HGTV and have a paint collection at Lowe's.

SHOPPE AMBER INTERIORS / shoppe.amberinteriordesign.com / various locations

F/D/L/R/A/C/T/B/V/K

When it comes to layering neutrals, Amber Lewis sets the bar! But don't take my word for it. Check out her storefront. Although most of her items are new, they have a relaxed, worn-in look and feel as if they've lived a previous gentle life. Fun fact: in 2020, Amber posted a photo of a bookcase that I styled, and my Instagram community rose by over 6K in one day. If you're reading this, Amber, thank you!

SOHO HOME / sohohome.com / various locations

F/D/L/R/A/C/T/B/K

It's no secret that I have a love affair with the brand of Soho House, a members-only club for creatives (think your dad's country club but with sneakers and T-shirts). They've now boxed up their eclectic London-born

vibe and put it into physical retail locations. The style is a mash-up of Victorian, mid-century modern, and rustic. You wouldn't think these styles would all work together, but somehow, they do. Pro tip: search online for the Soho Farmhouse for design inspiration. You can thank me later!

SOUTH LOOP LOFT / thesouthloploft.com / Chicago, Illinois

F/D/L/R/A/C/T/V

As this list goes on, I can't believe I am giving up all my best secret design resources. This vintage shop has a curated feel like someone has worked in visual marketing for years. From the window, you'll want to touch every object you see on the sales floor. Check out the lower levels on both sides of the store. This showroom also rents props to set decorators and home stagers.

STARK / starkcarpet.com / various locations

R

Stark is a veteran when it comes to rugs and carpets. Unlike several high-end shops, it has stacks of rugs that can be purchased on the same day without the annoyance of lead times.

STAYFOXX STUDIOS / stayfoxxstudios.com

A/D/C/V

In my quest to find unique abstract artwork that isn't mass-produced, I came across Kyle Boen's work. He offers a wide range of art mediums, and each piece is basically a "one and done," so you won't have to worry about everyone having your exact painting. He also carries several bespoke decorative accessories.

T

TAI PING CARPETS /
taipingcarpets.com

R

I often have clients with unique floor plans that can't accommodate a standard rectangular rug well. This showroom has a variety of organic rug styles that can be customized to your liking. They will also create a 3D drawing of your rug to help you pair the perfect colors.

TUFENKIAN ARTISAN CARPETS /
tufenkian.com / New York, New York

C

I fell in love with this carpet and rug showroom for my first designer showhouse. They have many tasteful rugs that can be customized to your specifications. Also, several of their showrooms have rugs you can take on the same day, which is rare in the world of high-end rugs. Pro tip: call their Chicago showroom to see if they have any rugs on sale that might not be listed online.

V

VISUAL COMFORT & CO. /
visualcomfort.com / various locations

L

Walking into one of these showrooms is like walking into a department store full of beautiful lighting. Each store is stocked with light fixtures that you are bound to see in almost every interior design magazine. They carry a range from traditional to modern lighting styles.

W

WEST ELM / westelm.com /
various locations

F/D/L/R/A/V/W/C/DH/WC/K

West Elm is perfect for finding stylish furniture and decor that really stands out. Their modern designs are all about clean lines and unique touches, making it easy to refresh your space. Plus, they often mix textures and colors in a new and inviting way.

WOODWARD THROWBACKS /
throwbackshome.com / Detroit, Michigan

F/D/L/A/V/C/K

Woodward Throwbacks is a fantastic spot in my hometown of Detroit that captures the city's rich history and vibrant culture. They offer an eclectic mix of vintage finds, locally crafted items, and salvaged and reclaimed products that tell a story. It's a great place to discover unique home decor and celebrate Detroit's creativity and community spirit!

THE WORKSHOP

F/D

This interior design firm creates custom furniture pieces. You can always count on their products to be modern yet not cold and sterile.

Y

YHD / yosemitehomedecor.com /
various locations

F/D/L/A

YHD is a fantastic spot where you can find my Mikel Welch Collection. The store features a carefully curated selection of stylish home decor and furniture that showcases a modern aesthetic. Fun fact: I got my furniture line after my mom popped into the store for a free gift bag, which turned into a great conversation with the VP. It perfectly exemplifies how unexpected moments can lead to exciting opportunities!

ACKNOWLEDGMENTS

It's always been a dream of mine to write a book, but I never really understood what it would take. It's more than just a collection of pretty photos; it's an explanation of my design methodology. As a creative, it can be hard to articulate why or how you do what you do. For me, as a self-taught designer, I've done everything based on a feeling rather than taking a technical approach. But composing this book taught me that I do, in fact, have a process; it just needed to be translated into words.

I want to first express my gratitude to my parents, Winston and Kathy Welch, for their unconditional love and support. I can recall my mother telling me to find my passion and that I would know what it was because it would be something that I'd be willing to do for free. And observing my father run several businesses gave me the entrepreneurial spirit needed to survive as an artist.

To my siblings, Keyon Chavis, David Welch, and Nicole Welch, thank you for being a sounding board and source of comfort. If I ever find myself in a jam, I can always count on you to rally together and back me up. Lurlean's favorite is grateful for you in so many ways and literally couldn't have pulled this book off without your assistance.

In life, you need a support system. These are the people you can call at three a.m. and who will run to assist you, no judgment or questions asked (well . . . maybe some judgment). Joseph Riley Land, Christian "Wiki" Allen, Pierre "Stick" Edwards, James Bianca, Vy'Shaey Mitchell, April Randall, and Chris and Dione Craft, I love you all dearly and can't wait to toast at the Soho Farmhouse.

When I reflect on my career, there are several people who encouraged me when I second-guessed myself and gave me the pep talks needed to move on. To my mentor, Jillian Browder, thank you for introducing me to the world of luxury design. Thank you for taking a chance on me and for your constant motivation and tough love. Kelli Bishop (Thelma and Louise), I can't thank you enough for teaching me the ropes of set design and, most important, Mastering Acorns and the art of BS. A huge part of my artistic journey has been in set design. I owe a huge acknowledgment to Jason Kurtz, Alex Duda, Kareen Gunning, Steve Harvey, Drew

Barrymore, Sedrick Hamilton, Rushion McDonald, Monica Barnes, Dejon Gee, Earl Nicholson, Kim Perel, Angelin Adams, Yasmeen Bandoo, Patricia Shaw, Kim Tyner, and everyone at Clarkson Potter, and Erin Austen Abbott. I also want to thank Sarah Jane Coolahan, Scott Feldman, Nazira Handal and the Kips Bay Designer Show House Committee, and Tony Manning and the Brooklyn Heights Designer Showhouse Committee. I've been continuously inspired by Shea and Syd McGee (thank you so much for writing a foreword for this book), Tawnee Walker, Jeanna George, Anita Yokota (I wouldn't have this book without you), Amber Lewis, Emily Henderson, Orlando Soria, Alvin Wayne, the Brownstone Boys (Barry and Jordan), Linda Hayslett, and Shauna Smith and the Inspired Closets team.

Last, I want to express my gratitude to my dog, Bailey, for sitting up with me every night as I penned this book.

I cherish you all!

PHOTO CREDITS

INDEX

Note: Page references in *italics*
indicate photographs.

A

Aaron, Ben, 20
Abalone color, 111
Abysse color, 108
Agreeable Gray color, 111
Alabaster color, 112
ambiance
    with art, 74–75
    in the bathroom, 56–61, 73
    in the bedroom, 54–55
    colors for, 47–48, 52
    creating, 42
    in the dining room, 62–65
    of hotels, 47
    lighting and, 42–43, 46–47, 52,
        66–70, 205
    plants for, 42–43, 47, 48, 49
    of restaurants, 62–65
    senses and, 47, 61
    symmetry in, 51–52
    texture for, 42–43
    theatrical design moments in, 71–72
    trial and error in, 77
    unexpected elements in, 77–80
    wallpaper for, 52
    wooden decor for, 44, 45
Ammonite color, 111
anchoring piece, 34, 35, 36. *See also*
    furnishings/furniture
Antoinette, Marie, 71
Architectural Digest (magazine), 20
architectural elements, 74–75, 77
art
    as anchor, 253
    in the bedroom, 75
    books as, 233
    color and, 88–89, 91, 245
    creation of, 77
    furniture as, 246–247
    for high ceilings, 253
    layering for, 246
    in the living room, 100, 252
    mirrors and, 246
    moving around, 250
    paint colors and, 245
    pairings for, 246
    power clashing, 245–246
    scaling, 225
    selecting, 245
    setting the mood with, 74–75
    tapestry as, 225
    as unexpected element, 78
art of the edit, 201

B

barn doors, 44
Barrymore, Drew, 21
baseboards, 102, 118
baskets, 249
bathroom
    ambiance in, 56–61, 73
    board-and-batten look for, 77
    colors for, 104
    drapery/window treatments for, 176
    hardware for, 56–57, 159
    re-creating hotel, 56–61
    satin sheen for, 101
    semigloss sheen for, 101
    theatrical moments in, 73
    tile for, 58
    unexpected elements in, 78
Bedrock color, 108
bedroom
    ambiance in, 54–55
    architectural elements of, 75
    artwork in, 75
    board-and-batten look for, 77
    color for, 83, 93, 94–95, 109, 114–115
    drapery/window treatments for, 184
    fabrics for, 55
    flat sheen for, 97
    furniture for, 195–197
    matte sheen for, 98
    rugs for, 150–153
    satin sheen for, 101
    semigloss sheen for, 101
    setting the mood in, 54–55
    texture for, 208
    theatrical moments in, 71, 75
Beetle Black color, 108
Berkus, Nate, 22
Berry, Halle, 22
binder, for space planning, 25–27,
    28, 38

Bishop-Pope, Kelli, 48
black color, 90, 108
Black Fox color, 111
Blackboard color, 108
Blondie color, 112
blue colors, 108
blue gray color, 90
blush pink color, 92
board-and-batten look, 77
books, as decor, 50, 233, 235–237,
    250
bookshelf, styling, 248–249
boutique hotel, incorporating looks of,
    47–48. *See also* hotel
Broadway color, 108
Browder, Jillian, 19
brown colors, 111
budget
    drapery/window treatments for, 176
    dumpster diving for, 22
    flooring for, 125
    for furnishings, 209
    luxury and, 42
    space planning for, 26

C

cabinets, 158–159, 160–163, 164, 166,
    221
café curtains, 176. *See also* drapery/
    window treatments
Cambridge color, 108
Canva, 28
cascading, 234–235, 249
ceiling, 35, 97, 98, 253
cellular shades, 180. *See also*
    drapery/window treatments
ceramic tile flooring, 133. *See also*
    floors/flooring
chandeliers, 66, 67. *See also* lighting/
    light fixtures
Chanel, Coco, 201
Chic Gray color, 111
china cabinet, as anchoring piece, 35
chocolate brown color, 90
climate, flooring and, 127, 133
clustering, 249
Coffee Date color, 111
coffee table, 233, 237

colors/paint colors
   of art, 88–89, 91, 245
   art and, 245
   autumn, 94
   in the bathroom, 104
   in the bedroom, 83, 93, 94–95, 109,
      114–115
   blacks, 108
   blues, 108
   brands of, 101
   brown, 111
   creating custom, 118
   for crown molding, 85
   dark and moody, 90, 94–95
   of decor, 88–89
   for doors, 94
   earth tones, 94
   eggshell sheen of, 98
   embracing, 105
   fashion as inspiration for, 94
   finding your true, 88–93
   flat sheen of, 97
   function of, 94
   furniture and, 85
   grays, 111
   greens, 112
   grout, 130
   for hallway, 105
   of hardware, 164
   importance of, 83
   in the kitchen, 113
   in the library, 84
   limewashing, 116–119
   in the living room, 86–87, 89,
      99–100, 106–107, 110, 116, 120
   matte sheen of, 94, 98
   monochromatic, 85–87
   mood board for, 94
   neutral, 82–83
   for open-concept areas, 105
   for pillows, 88–89
   power of, 94
   primer for, 102
   pushing boundaries of, 83
   satin sheen of, 101
   selecting, 245
   semigloss sheen of, 101
   for setting the mood, 47–48, 52
   sheen of, 97–101
   spray paint for, 102
   tried-and-true groupings of, 88
   whites, 112
concrete flooring, 133. See also floors/
   flooring

console table, 253
contracting, space planning for, 26
copper color, 90
Cornforth White color, 111
counterbalance, 237
Craigslist, 18, 221
cream color, 90, 92
Creamy Mushroom color, 111
creamy off-white color, 90
crown molding, 74, 85, 102, 118
Current Mood color, 112
curtain rods, 176. See also drapery/
   window treatments
curtains. See drapery/window
   treatments

D
Dakota Shadow color, 112
Dark as Night color, 112
Dark Ash color, 111
dark brown color, 90
dark cyan color, 92
Dark & Stormy color, 108
De Nimes color, 108
decluttering, 201, 203
decor
   artful arrangement of, 202–203
   books as, 50, 233, 235–237, 250
   for the coffee table, 233
   color and, 88–89
   communicating tastes through, 50
   counterbalance of, 237
   curating, 209
   in the dining room, 62–65
   in groups of three, 237
   imperfect items for, 74
   in the kitchen, 200–201
   layering, 228, 243
   for mantels, 243, 254
   mirror for, 204–205
   nestling of, 233
   pedestals for, 52–53, 55
   for shelves, 248–249
   taking time regarding, 201, 203
   vases as, 36–37, 76–77, 202–203,
      243
Decorations White color, 112
Deep Reddish Brown color, 111
design
   art of the edit in, 201
   changes to, 105
   getting started in, 201
   moments of pause in, 23

   taking time regarding, 203
   trial and error in, 77
design bible, 25–26, 36, 38
Design Star (television show), 20
details, emphasizing, 122
dining room, 62–65, 101, 146–149, 206,
   207
Dirty Chai color, 111
disc light, 205
doors, 94, 101, 118
The Double Red Duke (Clanfield,
   United Kingdom), 55
drama in design, 71–72
drapery/window treatments
   in the bathroom, 176
   in the bedroom, 184
   box pleat, 174
   budget for, 172, 176
   café curtains, 176, 178–179
   cellular shades, 180
   curtain rod for, 176
   goblet pleat, 174
   hard, 171
   hardware for, 180
   in the kitchen, 176, 178–179
   layered, 171
   in the living room, 170, 174, 177
   measuring for, 172
   overview of, 171, 172
   on panel track, 176
   pencil pleat, 174
   pinch pleat, 174
   preparing for, 180
   Roman shades, 180–183
   sheer curtains, 176
   shutters, 180
   single panel, 174
   soft, 171
   styles of, 171
   tab panel, 174
   tieback for, 174
Drawing Room color, 111
The Drew Barrymore Show (television
   show), 14, 15, 20, 21, 22, 205
drop cloths, 245
dumpster diving, 22

E
editing, 201
electricity, 26, 36, 205
Elle Decor (magazine), 20
engineered wood flooring, 125, 127,
   128–129. See also floors/flooring
entryway, 71, 159

Esquire Network, 20
Etsy, 223, 225
The Expert website, 22

F

fabric
  for the bedroom, 55
  care for, 190
  considerations regarding, 189
  eco-friendly, 189
  example of, 33
  for furniture, 188–189, 190, 192
  in high-traffic areas, 185
  in the living room, 186–188
  in low-traffic areas, 185
  outdoor, 185
  overview of, 185
  rub test for, 185
  selecting, 185
  slipcovers, 185, 190–191
  tried-and-true, 189
Facebook Marketplace, 221
family room, 101
fashion, as color inspiration, 94
faux limewash technique, 116–119
faux wood beams, 74–75
Fired Earth color, 111
fireplace, symmetry for, 51–52
floor lamp, 205. See also lighting/light
    fixtures
floors/flooring, 98, 125, 126–133
focal point, 201
forest green color, 90
forever home, 17, 22–23, 209
Four Seasons Hotel Miami (Florida),
    47, 55
French Beige color, 111
furnishings/furniture
  as anchoring piece, 34, 35, 36
  as art, 246–247
  in the bedroom, 195–197
  budget for, 209
  clearing room of, 28
  curating, 209
  fabric for, 188–189, 190, 192
  focal point for, 201
  harmony in, 209
  ins and outs of, 194
  layout for, 201
  lighting and, 66
  in the living room, 198–199
  overview of, 194
  paint colors and, 85
  painter's tape for, 32

photographing, 38
scale and, 35
space planning for, 28, 35, 36, 38
taking time regarding, 201, 203
texture of, 206
as unexpected element, 78–79

G

Gifford, Kathie Lee, 22
Good Jeans color, 108
Goodnight Moon color, 108
graph paper, for space planning, 36
Grate Black color, 108
gray colors, 111
green colors, 112
Greenland color, 112
grounding a room, 134
groups of three, 237
grout, 130

H

Hack My Home (television show), 20,
    233
haggling, 222
Hale Navy color, 108
Halloween, 205
hallway, 77, 101, 105
hardware
  backplates of, 166
  in the bathroom, 56–57, 159
  for cabinets, 158–159, 160–163, 164,
    166
  centering, 164–165
  color of, 164
  complementing space with, 164
  for doors, 94
  doubling up on, 159
  for drapery/window treatments, 180
  in the entryway, 159
  functionality of, 159
  guidelines for, 164
  in the kitchen, 158–159, 160–163,
    166, 167–168
  knobs, 160–163, 166
  of light fixtures, 72
  location of, 164–166
  materials in, 164
  overview of, 159
  preference of, 159
  pulls, 160–163, 166
  selecting, 159, 164, 166
  as unexpected element, 78
hardwood flooring, 126, 127. See also
    floors/flooring

Harry (television show), 20
Harvey, Steve, 122, 172, 209
height, overview of, 36
Henderson, Eily, 20
Henderson, Emily, 194
hidden-gem shops, 213–215
Highland color, 112
high-traffic areas, 35, 101, 154, 156, 185
Hill, Faith, 20, 25
home, function and purchase of, 17
hotels, 42, 47–48, 55, 56–61
The Hoxton, 55
Hughes, John, 20
humidity, flooring and, 127

I

illusion, art of, 23
Interior Motives color, 111

J

Jakes, T. D., 22
Jerseylicious (television show), 20

K

khaki/goldenrod color, 92
Kingsport Gray color, 111
Kismet color, 112
kitchen
  color for, 113
  considerations regarding, 221
  decor in, 200–201
  drapery/window treatments for, 176,
    178–179
  hardware in, 158–159, 160–163, 166,
    167–168
  layering in, 228
  rugs for, 154–155
  satin sheen for, 101
  semigloss sheen for, 101
  as workhorse of the home, 166
Kotb, Hoda, 22

L

laminate flooring, 129. See also floors/
    flooring
layering, 228, 243, 246
library, 84
light blue color, 92
Light color, 108
lighting/light fixtures
  ambiance and, 42–43, 46–47, 52,
    66–70, 205
  dark and moody, 205

lighting/light fixtures (*cont.*)
    dimmable, 47, 205
    disc light for, 205
    floor lamp, 205
    furniture and, 66
    hardware of, 72
    importance of, 66, 205
    intentionality for, 205
    mood and, 42–43
    natural, 36, 205
    pendant, 212–213
    planning grid for, 205
    puck light for, 205
    in restaurants, 66
    scale of, 35
    for setting the mood, 42–43, 46–47,
      52, 66–70, 205
    space planning for, 35
    triangular formation for, 205
    as unexpected element, 80
limewashing, 116–119
Lincoln Motor Company, 22
linoleum flooring, 133. *See also* floors/
    flooring
living room
    art in, 100, 252
    color for, 86–87, 89, 99–100,
      106–107, 110, 116, 120
    drapery/window treatments for, 170,
      174, 177
    fabrics for, 186–188
    flat sheen for, 97
    furniture for, 198–199
    matte sheen for, 98
    rugs for, 138–140, 141–145, 156–157
    satin sheen for, 101
    setting the mood in, 44, 46–47
    space planning for, 29
    unexpected elements in, 78–79
Locally Grown color, 112
low-traffic areas, 97, 185
luxury, in mood creation, 42
luxury vinyl flooring, 130. *See also*
    floors/flooring

M

mantels, 243, 246, 251, 254
The Martha Stewart Show (television
    show), 48
mauve color, 92
measuring, 28, 147, 172, 223
medium-tone blue color, 92
Mellow Mood color, 112
memories, re-creation of, 42

Mink Brown color, 111
mirror, 204–205, 246
Mirror Mirror color, 108
Mole's Breath color, 111
moments of pause, in design, 23
monochromatic rooms, 85–87
mood, 42–43, 47. *See also* ambiance;
    setting the mood
mood board, 24–25, 28, 94
Morning Ritual color, 112
moss, 78
muted purple color, 92

N

Narrows color, 111
The Nate Berkus Show (television
    show), 48
natural light, 36, 205. *See also*
    lighting/light fixtures
navy blue color, 90
The Ned Hotel (New York City, New
    York), 55
nestling, 233

O

Obama, Michelle, 22
ochre color, 90, 92
off-white/beige color, 90, 92
On Point color, 112
open-concept areas, 105

P

Paean Black color, 108
Pages, 28
painter's tape, 32, 35, 105, 156
paint/painting. *See also* colors/paint
    colors
    drop cloths and, 245
    example of, 33
    faux limewash technique in, 116–119
    painter's tape for, 105
    sponge, 105
    tips for, 98
    tools for, 102, 105, 117
    wallpaper and, 105
Palihouse, 55
panels, 223
pedestals, 52–53, 55
peel-and-stick materials, 169
Pepper Sam color, 108
Perry, Tyler, 22
Pickler, Kellie, 20
Pickler & Ben (television show), 20,
    25, 94

Pigeon color, 112
pillows, 88–89
Pinterest, 28, 74
planning, importance of, 25–27. *See
    also* space planning
Plano Room color, 112
plants
    for ambiance, 42–43, 47, 48, 49
    in the bedroom, 54–55
    faux, 48
    for high ceilings, 253
    scents of, 61
    for setting the mood, 42–43, 47, 48, 49
    for texture, 206
    for theatrical design moments, 71
    as unexpected element, 78–79
plum color, 90
Pointing color, 112
porcelain tile flooring, 133. *See also*
    floors/flooring
Port Blue color, 108
power clashing, 245–246
PowerPoint, 28
primer, 102
Project Runway (television show), 221
Property Brothers, 22
puck light, 205
Pure White color, 112

R

Railings color, 108
Rainy Days color, 108
The Real Housewives of Atlanta
    (television show), 20
renderings, 20, 28
renting, 25–26, 122, 134
restaurants, 42, 62–65, 66
reverse symmetry, 249
risk-taking, 19, 73, 83
Rivers, Joan, 22
Rolling Hills color, 112
Roman shades, 180–183. *See also*
    drapery/window treatments
Rooted in Comfort color, 112
rose color, 90
rub test, 185
rugs
    in the bedroom, 150–153
    benefits of, 151
    choosing, 122
    considerations regarding, 121–122
    cotton, 156
    in the dining room, 146–149
    example of, 33

in the kitchen, 154–155
layering, 154
in the living room, 138–140, 141–145, 156–157
materials of, 154
measuring for, 147
natural fibers of, 154
overview of, 134
pads for, 156
painter's tape for, 156
pile of, 156
runners as, 154
scale and, 137
selecting, 134–135
silk, 156
space planning for, 32
synthetic fibers of, 154, 156
texture of, 136, 154, 156
wool, 156
woven, 156–157
runners, 154

S

sage green color, 92
salmon color, 92
scale, 35, 36, 137, 225, 253
scents, incorporation of, 61
School House White color, 112
screenshots, for space planning, 38
sculptures, 202–203, 243
Secrets from a Stylist (television show), 20
senses, 47, 61
Sentimental Reasons color, 111
setting the mood
    ambiance creation for, 42
    with art, 74–75
    in the bathroom, 56–61, 73
    in the bedroom, 54–55
    with board-and-batten look, 77
    colors for, 47–48, 52
    in the dining room, 62–65
    lighting and, 42–43, 46–47, 52, 66–70, 205
    in the living room, 44, 46–47
    pedestals for, 52–53, 55
    plants for, 42–43, 47, 48, 49
    restaurants and, 62–65
    with scents, 61
    symmetry in, 51–52
    texture for, 42–43
    theatrical design moments in, 71–72
    trial and error in, 77
    unexpected elements in, 77–80

wallpaper for, 52
    wooden decor for, 44, 45
sheen, paint, 97–101
sheer curtains, 176. *See also* drapery/window treatments
shelves, 51–52, 248–249
showhouses, 19–20
shutters, 180. *See also* drapery/window treatments
Silhouette color, 111
Silver Lake Dad color, 111
slipcovers, 185, 190–191
Smokestack Gray color, 108
smoky gray color, 90
Snowbound color, 112
sofa, space planning for, 26, 28, 32, 36. *See also* furnishings/furniture
Soho Farmhouse (Oxfordshire, United Kingdom), 55
Soot color, 108
space planning
    binder for, 25–27, 28
    Canva for, 28
    for ceiling height, 35
    clearing room for, 28
    considerations in, 36
    design bible for, 25–26, 36
    elements of, 26–27
    existing features for, 28
    getting started in, 28, 32
    graph paper for, 36
    height in, 36
    as home*work,* 27
    importance of, 25–27
    layouts testing in, 32
    measuring for, 28, 36
    mood board for, 24–25
    natural light considerations in, 36
    organization of, 28
    Pages for, 28
    painter's tape for, 32, 35
    Pinterest for, 28
    PowerPoint for, 28
    screenshots for, 38
    to stay on budget, 26
    to stay on task, 26
    tools for, 28, 38
    variables consideration in, 28
    visual representation for, 28
    visualizing in, 32
    to work smarter, 26–27
sponge-painting, 105
spray paint, 102
Starless Sky color, 108, 111

The Steve Harvey Show (television show), 20
Stewart, Martha, 22
stone color, 92
stone flooring, 130. *See also* floors/flooring
Stonecraft color, 112
Sunbrella, 185
Swiss Coffee color, 112
symmetry, 51–52

T

tan/beige color, 90
tape measure, 26. *See also* measuring
tapestry, 74, 225
Teen Vogue (magazine), 20
television, 26, 35
terra-cotta color, 92
texture, 42–43, 136, 154, 206, 207, 208
theatrical moments, 71–72, 74–75, 76–77
thrifting, 34–35, 38–40, 221–223
tile, 58, 78, 169
Timeless color, 112
Trading Spaces (television show), 20
Tricom Black color, 108
trim, 101, 118

V

vases, 36–37, 76–77, 202–203, 243
vintage decor, thrifting for, 38–40. *See also* decor
vinyl flooring, 130. *See also* floors/flooring
visualizing, for space planning, 32
visuals, 20, 28

W

wallpaper, 52, 105, 169
walls, measuring, 28
Washi color, 111
waterfall effect, 234–235, 249, 253
Wellfleet color, 108
white colors, 112
white/off-white color, 90
Whitfield, Shereé, 20
window treatments. *See* drapery/window treatments
windows, 28, 36, 101. *See also* drapery/window treatments
wine red color, 92
Winfrey, Oprah, 22
wood beams, 74–75
wooden decor, 44, 45. *See also* decor

CLARKSON POTTER/PUBLISHERS
An imprint of the Crown Publishing Group
A division of Penguin Random House LLC
1745 Broadway
New York, NY 10019
clarksonpotter.com
penguinrandomhouse.com

Library of Congress Cataloging-in-Publication Data
is available upon request.

ISBN 978-0-593-79693-1
Ebook ISBN 978-0-593-79694-8

Additional credits appear on page 266.

Editor: Angelin Adams | Editorial assistant: Darian Keels
Designer: Yasmeen Bandoo | Design manager: Ian Dingman
Production designer: Christina Self
Production editor: Patricia Shaw
Production: Kim Tyner
Compositors: Merri Ann Morrell, Zoe Tokushige, and
Hannah Hunt
Copy editor: Sibylle Kazeroid | Proofreaders: Alissa
Fitzgerald, Sigi Nacson, and Tricia Wygal
Indexer: Elise Hess
Publicist: Lauren Chung | Marketer: Joey Lozada

Manufactured in China

10 9 8 7 6 5 4 3 2 1

First Edition

The authorized representative in the EU for product
safety and compliance is Penguin Random House Ireland,
Morrison Chambers, 32 Nassau Street, Dublin D02 YH68,
Ireland, https://eu-contact.penguin.ie.